D1404292

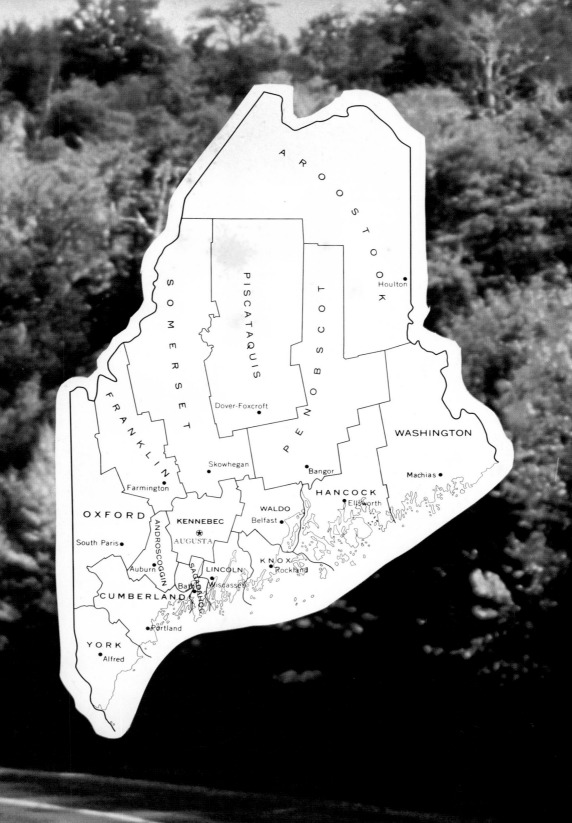

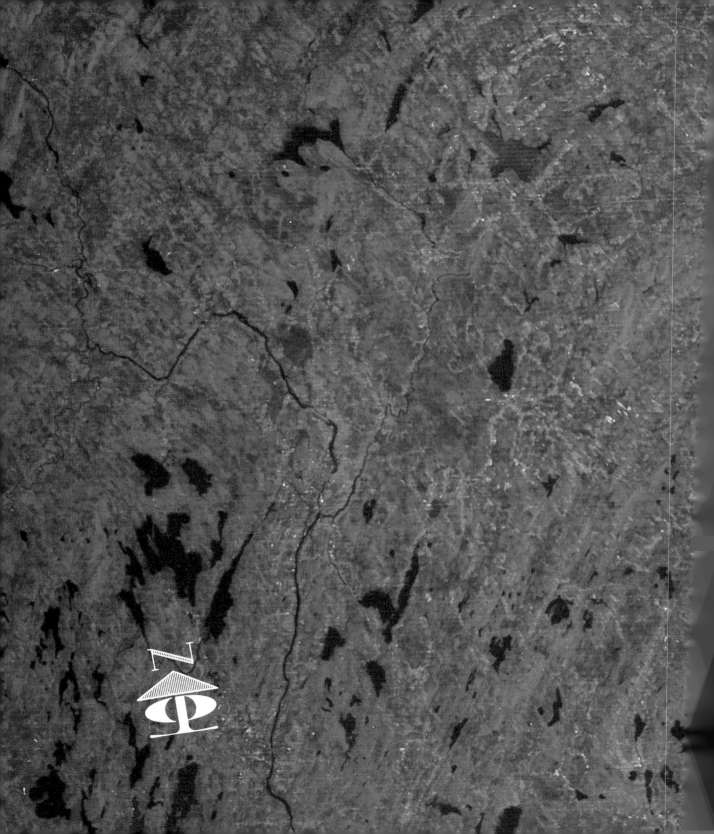

The New
Enchantment of America
MAINE

By Allan Carpenter

 CHILDRENS PRESS, CHICAGO

ACKNOWLEDGMENTS

For assistance in the preparation of the revised edition, the author thanks:
ALVAR LAIHO, Deputy Director, Maine State Development Office, Augusta.

American Airlines—Anne Vitaliano, Director of Public Relations; *Capitol Historical Society*, Washington, D. C. ; *Newberry Library*, Chicago, Dr. Lawrence Towner, Director; *Northwestern University Library*, Evanston, Illinois; *United Airlines*—John P. Grember, Manager of Special Promotions; Joseph P. Hopkins, Manager, News Bureau; Carl Provorse, *Carpenter Publishing House.*

UNITED STATES GOVERNMENT AGENCIES: *Department of Agriculture*—Robert Hailstock, Jr., Photography Division, Office of Communication; Donald C. Schuhart, Information Division, Soil Conservation Service. *Army*—Doran Topolosky, Public Affairs Office, Chief of Engineers, Corps of Engineers. *Department of Interior*—Louis Churchville, Director of Communications; EROS Space Program—Phillis Wiepking, Community Affairs; Charles Withington, Geologist; Mrs. Ruth Herbert, Information Specialist; Bureau of Reclamation; National Park Service—Fred Bell and the individual sites; Fish and Wildlife Service—Bob Hines, Public Affairs Office. *Library of Congress*—Dr. Alan Fern, Director of the Department of Research; Sara Wallace, Director of Publications; Dr. Walter W. Ristow, Chief, Geography and Map Division; Herbert Sandborn, Exhibits Officer. *National Archives*—Dr. James B. Rhoads, Archivist of the United States; Albert Meisel, Assistant Archivist for Educational Programs; David Eggenberger, Publications Director; Bill Leary, Still Picture Reference; James Moore, Audio-Visual Archives. *United States Postal Service*—Herb Harris, Stamps Division.

For assistance in the preparation of the first edition, the author thanks:
Mary Woodman, Director of Public Relations, The Maine Teachers Association; Laurence Bagley, Director of Field Services, The Maine Teachers Association; John H. Reed, former governor; Clyde Russell, Executive Secretary, The Maine Teachers Association; Department of Economic Development, State of Maine; Maine Historical Society; Greater Portland Chamber of Commerce.

Illustrations on the preceding pages:
Cover photograph: Stonington, Margrit Fiddle
Page 1: Commemorative stamps of historic interest
Pages 2-3: A country road in fall, Maine State Development Office
Page 3: (Map) USDI Geological Survey
Pages 4-5: Bangor-Waterville-Augusta-Lewiston area, EROS Space Photo, USDI Geological Survey, EROS Data Center

Project Editor, Revised Edition:
  Joan Downing
Assistant Editor, Revised Edition:
  Mary Reidy

Library of Congress Cataloging in Publication Data

Carpenter, John Allan, 1917-
  Maine.

  (His The new enchantment of America)
  SUMMARY: A presentation of the Pine Tree State, including its history, resources, famous citizens, and places of interest.
  [1. Maine] 1. Maine—Juvenile literature. I. Title. II. Series.
  F19.3.C3   1979   974.1   79-10804
  ISBN 0-516-04119-3

Contents

A True Story to Set the Scene

VIRGINIA OF SAGADAHOC

It was a small crowd that had gathered at the mouth of the Kennebec River where it flows along the Sagadahoc Peninsula. The people there could not have realized that the event they were about to witness might someday be considered important. Nevertheless, they were tremendously interested.

Occasionally the ring of a spike maul sounded in the autumn air as a hammer struck against soft iron. The muffled chunk-chunk sound of dubbing adzes could be heard as a few of the last rough wood surfaces were chopped smooth.

Finally, all was ready! Holding blocks were knocked away. After a breathless period, when the people saw that everything had gone smoothly, a thin but hearty cry went up from those on the riverbank as the first ship in the New World was launched.

The year was 1607; George Popham and Raleigh Gilbert had brought a group of about 120 settlers to establish the first English colony in Maine. They arrived at the mouth of the Kennebec on August 19 in two ships, the *Gift of God* and the *Mary and John*. They called their settlement, near present-day Popham, St. George. In the short time the colony survived, its members were able to build shelters, construct a fort with twelve cannon, and erect a church.

Even more incredible is the fact that within two days after they landed, Digby, an experienced shipbuilder from London, had assembled a number of men who were familiar with shipbuilding and had crews at work in the forest cutting the fine Maine timbers to construct a ship.

Even more difficult to comprehend is how the men could have built a ship and launched it in early September—only two or three weeks after the work was begun. However, marine expert William Hutchinson Rowe contends this was definitely possible, because a

Opposite: Building the famed yacht America *at East Boothbay carries on the tradition of the hemisphere's first ship.*

drawing made by one of the colonists on September 8 shows the new ship at anchor under the guns of the fort.

Whatever the date, there is no doubt that the vessel, the *Virginia,* actually slid down the crude log ways and splashed into the waters of the Kennebec fairly early in the colony's existence. The proud leader of the colony was able to write in his canvas-covered journal for 1607: "Virginia launched this day; a fair pynnace of thirty tons burthen . . . George Popham, Master." This 30-ton (27-metric ton) ship was also 30 feet (9 meters) long, had a beam of 13 feet (4 meters) and drew 8 feet (2.4 meters) of water. According to the *Maine Book,* by Henry Ernest Dunnack, the colonists sacrificed their shirts to make the first sails for the craft.

In that same book, Dunnack calls it "the first ship built by European hands" on the continent. Another expert, Reese Wolfe, goes even further, pointing out that although there may have been ships built by Dutch, French, or Spanish explorers in the New World before the *Virginia,* there are no records of them. Wolfe hails the ship as "the first ocean-going vessel to be launched in America."

The *Virginia* made several trips up and down the river on fur-collecting expeditions. It made at least one voyage to newly established Jamestown, Virginia, with a load of salted codfish. However, the Maine winter of 1607-1608 was particularly severe. Popham and many of the other settlers died and, sadly, the St. George colony was abandoned. Those who survived sailed back to England. The *Virginia,* filled with furs and sassafras which brought a fortune to the backers of the colony who had remained in England, arrived safely after the long voyage to Plymouth, England.

For twenty years the *Virginia* sailed the seas—a tribute to the indomitable men who built it in a rugged wilderness. At last, Wolfe says, it fell, a "victim in a lonely stretch of another sea, to the Barbary Pirates." According to an entirely different version by Rowe, "She was wrecked on the Irish coast" while returning to England from Virginia with a load of tobacco.

Whatever its fate, the *Virginia* will always be remembered as one of Maine's extraordinary accomplishments, a tribute to the persistence, courage, and ingenuity typical of the Maine character.

Lay of the Land

MAINE GREETS THE MORNING

When the sun lifts its first arc above the horizon, the light sparkles on the state of Maine, and morning begins for the United States. A point in Maine is the first in all the fifty states to greet the morning sun. The location of the particular spot is said to vary with the season.

Maine boasts the most easterly point in the continental United States, and by some turnabout of logic this is known as West Quoddy Head.

Maine is the largest of all the New England states. Its area of 33,215 square miles (86,026 square kilometers) makes Maine almost as large as all of the other New England states combined. Aroostook County is larger than the states of Connecticut and Rhode Island. Maine is the only state with just one other state—New Hampshire—on its boundary. Canada and the ocean are its other boundaries.

"HUNDRED-HARBORED MAINE"

If a master designer and builder set out to create the world's most dramatic, interesting, and unusual seashore, the results would probably resemble the coast of Maine. This splendid meeting of water and land is perhaps the outstanding single physical feature of Maine.

The highest tides of the continental United States and Canada sweep into Passamaquoddy Bay, sometimes pushing their surging waters up the foot of Quoddy Head to a height of 28 feet (8.5 meters). In some of the coastal rivers, the tides are felt 40 miles (64 kilometers) upstream.

Much of the Maine shore is indeed "rockbound" as tradition says, but there are also miles of sunny, sandy beaches plus gemlike islands by the hundreds.

Dominating Maine's multitude of islands is Mount Desert Isle,

described as "one of the most dramatically beautiful spots in the entire world." After Long Island, New York, it is the largest island on the Atlantic coast of the United States. Mount Desert's wooded acres encompass twenty-six lakes and ponds, and it has the highest elevation of all the islands on the coast, with eighteen "mountains."

Cadillac Mountain, on the island, soars from the surf to a height of 1,532 feet (467 meters). It is the highest point on the Atlantic coast north of Rio de Janeiro in Brazil. From its lofty summit, there is a breathtaking panorama of ocean, mountains, lakes, and islands.

Casco Bay is dotted with picturesque isles and islets. In fact, in the bay there is said to be an "island a day"—365 in all—so they are called the Calendar Islands. Monhegan Island, off Boothbay Harbor, is known as the Sentinel of New England. Another picturesque island group is the Cranberry Islands. Vinalhaven, North Haven, Deer Isle, Isle au Haut, and Swans Island are some of the larger offshore islands.

Sometimes the many rocks and islets are a hazard to navigation. This was true of Cushnoc Island in the Kennebec River at Augusta, and an interesting sidelight resulted. In about 1820, planners of the area decided to haul the island out of the river. They attached a hundred yoke of oxen to it with enormous chains. The two hundred panting and snorting beasts dug their hoofs into the ground and pulled with such a mighty tug that the rear teams were thrown into the water. In spite of a day's straining and shouting, the island remained just as it was.

Someone has said that the shoreline east of Portland is similar to that of Norway. Bold headlands with deep bays that stretch far back to the forested hills and mountains remind world travelers of Norway's fjords. If Viking explorers really did visit these coasts, they must have felt right at home.

Penobscot is the largest of all Maine bays; it has been labeled one of the most picturesque coastlines in the world. Other bays are Passamaquoddy (most of which is in Canada), Casco, Machias, Englishman, Pleasant, Frenchman, and Muscongus.

Opposite: Acadia National Park.

Nubble Lighthouse, York.

If these and all the other indentations on the coast were stretched into a straight line, they would reach for almost 3,500 miles (5,633 kilometers), which is the actual length of Maine's rockbound shoreline. However, the coastline extends about 250 miles (402 kilometers) as the crow flies.

MIGHTY WATERS

Three rivers on the United States Geologic Survey of principal rivers of the United States flow their entire length or almost their entire length within Maine's borders: the Androscoggin, the Kennebec, and the Penobscot. Other principal rivers of Maine are the St. John and the St. Croix, both of which help to outline part of the state's border with Canada. The St. John River takes a most unusual course, flowing north, east, and finally south. The Kennebec is one of the historic rivers of the continent. It was among the first streams to be explored along the coast of North America.

Altogether, there are more than five thousand rivers and streams flowing through Maine. The Saco River was immortalized in poems by both Henry Wadsworth Longfellow and John Greenleaf Whittier.

14

It rises in New Hampshire and follows a long path through Maine. The Allagash River is noted for its canoe trips and rapids. The Nonesuch River takes its name because its course is so crooked it hardly seemed possible that such a river could exist. Moose River is the largest feeder of Moosehead Lake.

The Kennebec and Androscoggin rivers converge in a way that is probably unique among major rivers of the world. They come together almost directly facing each other, and the Kennebec continues on to the sea. Geologists think that the Androscoggin once emptied directly into Casco Bay but that silt clogged up its former mouth and a new channel was carved to meet the Kennebec.

Most of the coastal rivers of Maine end in what is known as drowned valleys. These once were dry land but were flooded when the ocean levels rose after glaciers of the Ice Ages melted.

Maine is blessed with more than six thousand crystal clear lakes and ponds. Largest of these is mighty Moosehead Lake. With its 300-mile (483-kilometer) long shoreline, Moosehead seems to

Camden's harbor is much like those found in other parts of Maine.

15

many people to be more like an arm of the ocean than a lake, although it is 1,000 feet (305 meters) above sea level.

Sebago Lake, with its fourteen Dingley Islands, is one of the state's larger, popular lakes. The six Rangeley lakes and the six Belgrade lakes are popular chains of lakes. Many other lakes are notable for their size, popularity, and sometimes their strange-sounding Indian names: Pemadumcook, Chesuncook, Chemquasabamticook, Mooselookmeguntic, Pennesseewassee, Umbagog, Graham, and two Grand lakes, among hundreds of others. Two adjacent lakes bear names of men who also were placed together in historical chronology—Chamberlain and Churchill. Popular lakes near the city of Augusta are Maranacook, Annabessacook, and Cobbosseecontee.

"GIANTS OF THE EAST"—THE MOUNTAINS

There are ten mountains in Maine that are more than 4,000 feet (1,219 meters) in height. The northernmost section of the Appalachian Mountains, which runs through Maine, is known as the Longfellow Mountains. The mighty monarch of the Longfellow Mountains, the highest point in Maine, is Mount Katahdin, rising majestically to 5,267 feet (1,605 meters). This isolated, gray granite monolith takes its name from the Indian term *Kette adene,* meaning "greatest mountain."

According to Indian legend, Mount Katahdin was created by the Council of the Gods as a sacred meeting place. The gods refused to seat Pamola, a lesser god, at their councils. In great anger he is said to have gone to one of the other peaks of Katahdin, now called Pamola Peak. The Indians believed he took out his anger on anyone who ventured near Mount Katahdin. Even today when storm clouds glower on the summit and the wind swirls across the Knife Edge, Pamola is said to be showing his anger.

The summit of Mount Katahdin is called Baxter Peak in honor of Percival P. Baxter, who gave to the state of Maine the mountain and most of what is now known as Baxter State Park, so that, as Mr. Bax-

Sugarloaf Mountain is a skiers' paradise.

ter wrote: "Katahdin in its grandeur will forever remain the mountain of the people of Maine."

Sugarloaf Mountain is the second highest in Maine. Picturesque place names have also been applied to such mountains as Quoggy Joe. One of the most unusual peaks in Maine is known as Mount Kineo. It rises 1,806 feet (550 meters) out of the very center of Moosehead Lake.

THE LAND—YESTERDAY AND TODAY

Sandstone, shale, and limestone form the bedrock of Maine, and these were formed in the geologic eras known as Precambrian and Paleozoic. At various times great masses of granite called batholiths pushed their way upward. Grimy looking masses of ash and lava were left by ancient volcanoes. Mount Kineo is the best known of

17

the lava formations. Mountain ranges rose and sank over vast ages of time.

As the glaciers of the Ice Age scoured their way across what is now Maine, they drastically changed the face of the land. They leveled off hills, gouged out holes where most of Maine's lakes would form, and left dams of earth and rock which later created other lakes when the vast weight of ice finally melted. Rivers were forced from their courses by the glaciers and in many cases made to flow through narrow gorges and over high falls.

The melting glaciers left many mounds and ridges of dirt, sand, and rocks called moraines. Hogback ridges are moraines of gravel, some only a mile (1.6 kilometers) long, some as much as 150 miles (241 kilometers) in length. In some areas the glaciers left large quantities of sand. Near Freeport this sand was carried by the winds to form an unusual region that is now known as the "desert of Maine." The desert began as a patch of sand about thirty feet (nine meters) across. Today, it covers several hundred acres, burying everything in its path. Tops of tall trees, still growing, look like bushes, and one buried apple tree blossomed and bore fruit on its uncovered branches for many years.

The present topography of Maine might be generally described as a broad plateau, sloping southeastward until it meets the Atlantic Ocean. Out of this plateau rise the mountains, and in its broad expanse are clustered the many lakes.

CLIMATE

Maine's evenly distributed rainfall averages 43.24 inches (110 centimeters) a year, including snow equal to 6.91 inches (17.5 centimeters) of rain. Serious drought or heavy storms are exceedingly rare, as are tornados, severe blizzards, and hurricanes. The lack of storms greatly enhances the livability of the state. The winters are less severe than those in interior states the same distance north. Winter air is dry and clear. Summer days are pleasant; nights are delightfully cool; and autumn weather is quite invigorating.

18

Footsteps on the Land

PEOPLE OF THE RED PAINT

The body was placed carefully in its final resting place; around it were laid all the implements the deceased might need in the after-world. There were fire-making stones, sturdy flint knives, carefully chipped adze blades, projectile points, and sharpening stones. Then, around the body was laid almost a bushel of powder of a brilliant red color. Over everything was heaped a pile of great rocks to form a strong tomb.

Such burial scenes must have been fairly common at some unknown time thousands of years ago in what is now the state of Maine. However, who the people were who made such burials, where they came from and what happened to them are still unknown. These ancient people who lived at least five thousand years ago are known today as the Red Paint People, because of the brilliant red ochre powder found in their graves.

Some experts feel the Red Paint People may have been of Eskimo background, while others think that they might have come from Newfoundland. Were they the ancestors of Indians found in Maine during historic times? No one knows. From the many items the Red Paint People left behind it appears that they may have been very skillful artisans, although they apparently were not aware of the bow and arrow. The Red Paint People did construct a wooden canoe of some type. Five hundred great heaps of shells dating from one thousand to five thousand years ago indicate that they enjoyed seafood in their diet.

Most of the graves of the Red Paint People have been found beside the water, including those at Hampden, Howland, Milford, Eddington, Swanville, Bradley, Old Town, Bucksport, Passadumkeag, Orland, Waterville, Kineo, Oakland, Winslow, and other places in Maine. Despite these discoveries, the true facts about these people remain one of the great mysteries of archaeology.

LAND OF THE ABNAKI AND ETCHIMIN

The earliest European visitors to what is now Maine found that the Indians there belonged to two major divisions of the great Algonquin nation: the Abnaki, who lived west of the Penobscot River, and the Etchimin, who lived to the east. These people were so closely related that a good deal of confusion has resulted regarding their tribal names and descriptions. One recognized authority states that there were about twenty tribes of Abnaki, with four major divisions—Saco, Anasagunticook, Kennebec, and Wawenock.

The word Etchimin means "the men," and they appeared to be seafaring tribes. Their three principal bands—Penobscot, Pentagoet, and Passamaquoddy—all spoke a similar dialect. Passamaquoddy means "people who spear pollock."

In June their campsites would probably be placed on the seashore. There the men cleverly hunted porpoise and seal. The women processed the oil and skins and used the skins for clothing, containers, and other necessities. The boys searched for bird eggs and learned the ways of hunting by craftily snaring sea birds.

The frosts of September called the Etchimin back to the riverbanks where they had planted crops earlier. After the harvests they went farther inland to hunt fall game. Ready at last for winter, they generally celebrated a two-week thanksgiving period, feasting on cranberries, turkey, and Indian pudding, much as their present-day imitators do. Winter found them in the deep woods, hunting moose and setting traps for fur bearers, such as otter and beaver.

Then, as spring came, the canoes were hauled out and used for spearhunting the wily muskrat, followed by a return to the river banks where the women could do the spring planting.

Besides the skills of hunting, stalking, trapping, fishing, and canoeing, the Indians were experts in drying and curing food, tanning hides, and sewing and making moccasins, fish nets, bows and arrows, spears, wampum, pottery, canoes, and snowshoes. In addition to necessities, they fashioned intricate clothing ornaments from dried quills, colored and threaded on leather thongs. They created carved pipes, and wove splendid baskets from flexible strips of brown ash, or sometimes basswood and sweet-grass. The Indians also had a knowledge of many useful herbs and medicines.

Related tribes and families often made extended visits with one another and appeared to enjoy close association with their large groups of relatives. Indians of Maine were usually gentle people.

A LEIF FROM THE VIKING BOOK

Did the dauntless prow of some tiny Viking ship once push through the morning mists to discharge its passengers on the Maine shore more than a thousand years ago? Were the Norsemen met by other little-known figures, ancestors of the later Indians?

There has long been speculation that Leif the Lucky, son of Eric the Red, had reached the coast of North America and had explored it

"Leiv Eriksson Discovers America," by Per Krohg (1936)
after Christian Krohg (1893).

thoroughly in the years 1000, 1003, 1006, 1007, and 1011. If he did so, he must certainly have touched at some time what is present-day Maine. Other Norse navigators may have done so also.

Because of recent discoveries, these epics of the past seem much more likely, even probable, but the records of history still bear no positive proof of Viking exploration.

Almost as strange is the belief of some that Portuguese fishermen enjoyed the fine fishing in the waters off Monhegan Island even before Columbus made his first voyage. Here, again, nothing positive is known.

However, it is known that King Henry VII of England sent John Cabot and his sons Sebastian, Sanctus, and Lewis in 1497 to "discover and occupy isles of countries of the heathen or infidels before unknown to Christians." The Cabots claimed to have explored the present New England coastline thoroughly, and it was upon this voyage that England based most of its later claims to the New World.

In 1524 an Italian explorer employed by the French, Giovanni de Verrazano, came to the Maine coast, followed in the next year by Gomez, a Spaniard. In 1527 or about that time, master French pilot Jean Allefonsce described a cape and river which he called Norumbega, now thought to be the Penobscot. Norumbega, a mythical city of folklore, was said to be so wealthy that its magnificent buildings were supported on pillars of silver and crystal. For many years it was thought to exist somewhere in the Penobscot region.

Probably the first Europeans to travel inland in what is now Maine were three English sailors who in 1568 had been put ashore by Sir John Hawkins on the Gulf of Mexico. They headed north on foot, and after an extraordinary journey arrived at the far-off soil of what is now Maine. The men were rather vague on their exact adventures, but one of them, David Ingram, was the author of an imaginative and popular account in which he claimed to have visited the city of Norumbega.

Other explorers and probably many adventurous fishermen sailed the waters off Maine during the late 1500s and early 1600s. A careful study of the Maine coast from the Piscataqua to the Penobscot was made by Martin Pring in 1603.

BEGINNINGS

French aristocrat Pierre du Guast, the Sieur de Monts, received trading rights to a vast area of the North American coast. In 1604 he landed at a place now known as Dochet Island, accompanied by seventy-nine colonists, including a Huguenot minister and a Catholic priest. He called the place St. Croix. So little was known about the region that they brought with them timber to use in construction. With the vast forests all around, they soon found that bringing wood to Maine was a most useless endeavor.

Du Guast's lieutenant was a man who later became one of the most noted explorers in the New World—Samuel de Champlain. The men created the earliest European settlement in what is now Maine, building barracks, dining hall, kitchen, storehouse, and blacksmith shop. Champlain did much exploring and investigating. In September he sailed up the Penobscot to the present site of Bangor and found the region "most pleasant and agreeable." After exploring a large island, he wrote: "I named it Isle des Monts Deserts." Champlain always treated the Indians with great courtesy and respect. He laid the basis for the great and lasting friendship of the Indians for the French. Father Nichols d'Aubri preached to the Indians at St. Croix and was Maine's first Christian Missionary.

That Christmas the little St. Croix settlement celebrated as best it could, but the winter was a difficult one and there was much sickness. The short-lived settlement was moved to Nova Scotia in 1605. Much later it would play an interesting and unusual part in saving a large part of Maine for the United States.

During an exploration of 1605, George Waymouth planted a cross on Allen Island to establish the English claim to the region. He and his party traded with the Indians in a friendly manner, receiving valuable furs for trinkets. Then suddenly he seized and kidnapped five Indians—Amoret, Tahanedo, Maneddo, Skicoworos, and Saffacomoit. When they were brought to England, they attracted much attention and provided valuable information about the New World. However, much of the Indian hatred of the English in the region dated from Waymouth's unfortunate hostile act.

As already mentioned, the first English settlement in what is now Maine was the Popham colony. With them the Popham colonists brought back one of the kidnapped Indians—Skicoworos—to America. They had first landed on Allen Island in August 1607, where the party held a "praise service" for the safe voyage. This is called by some "New England's first thanksgiving."

In 1609 Henry Hudson visited Maine, robbing friendly Indians who had been kind to him, and they in turn drove him away. In a different spirit, the devoted Jesuits established the first monastery-mission east of California in Maine in 1613. They later were driven out by the English.

Captain John Smith from the Jamestown colony carried his exploration activities even farther north—finally arriving in Maine in 1614. He and his men planted a garden on Monhegan Island which, as he said, "served us for salads." He also established fisheries on the island for the benefit of the Virginia colonies. Christmas Cove was given that name by Smith on Christmas Day 1614. In describing Maine, he wrote: "Those barren Isles are so furnished with good woods, springs, fruits, fish and foule, that it makes me think though the coast be rocky, and thus affrightable, the valleys, plains, and interior parts may well be very fertile."

Captain Smith also gave the name Boston to the area now known as York, providing a Boston in Maine sixteen years before the more famous one was founded in Massachusetts.

Although there were no settlements at this time that would become permanent, many traders, trappers, and fishermen practiced their trade. Pemaquid was a thriving trading post for business in furs. When the Pilgrims of Plymouth, Massachusetts, suffered such bitter hardships in the winter of 1620-1621, the European fishermen and traders and the Indians of Maine helped them with supplies and food. It might almost be said the Indians kept the Plymouth settlers' alive by advising them on how to get through a New England winter and giving of their own bounty.

One of the most benevolent of the Indians was the great Maine Indian leader Samoset, the *sagamore* (chief) described by one settler as a "magnificent figure, tall and straight."

Rock-strewn coast, Acadia National Park.

MAIN, MAYN, MAYNE

In 1622 Sir Ferdinando Gorges and Captain John Mason were given a vast grant in New England. The papers completing this grant said that Gorges and Mason "Intend to call the Province of Maine." It has been known also as Main, Mayn, and Mayne, among other names. In that year Maine's first permanent settlement, Monhegan, was established, followed by Saco in 1623 and York, settled in 1624 by the Plymouth colony. It was then known as Agamenticus.

The city of Portland was founded by George Cleve and Richard Tucker in 1633; it was then known as Machigonne. In 1642 York became the first city to be chartered in America. During this period the thriving fur trade was most important to the region's residents. The Plymouth Pilgrims received Maine trading rights and paid the debts of the Mayflower journey with the profits from Maine furs. The "fur trail" from Canada to Portland, entering through the Androscoggin Valley west of present-day Bethel, became well established. Fortunes also were made in sassafras and other goods.

In 1652 the Maine region was taken under the supervision of the colony of Massachusetts, and in 1658 the southern section of the province of Maine became the Massachusetts county of Yorkshire. Massachusetts gained a clear English title to much of Maine in 1677, when the Gorges heirs sold their rights. However, when King Charles II of England ceded Nova Scotia to France, the French claimed that this cession included all the province of Maine and that the French had also laid claim to it since 1667. The gallant young Baron de St. Castin became an important figure in Maine for more than thirty years, protecting French interests in the area and yet not overlooking the advantages of trading with the English as well. He married an Indian princess.

INDIANS, ENGLISH, AND FRENCH

By 1675 there were about six thousand European settlers in what is now Maine. The French continued to treat the Indians with consideration; French Catholic missionaries labored under conditions of great sacrifice among the Indians. Father Gabriel Druillettes had been a pioneer Indian missionary. At a later period Father Sebastian Rasle, a devoted worker among the Indians, became a martyr, murdered by the English. They also took the dictionary of the Abnaki language on which Father Rasle had labored. The Abnaki were among the first Indians in North America to accept Christianity.

26

The Indians had been generally friendly to the Europeans, and probably most of the English settlers treated them well. But others betrayed their confidence; Indians were cheated, insulted, and assaulted. The story is told that in 1675 a party of English sailors was rowing on the Saco River. When they saw an Indian woman in a canoe with her infant, they decided to test the legend that Indian children could swim from the day they were born, and they overturned the canoe. The mother saved herself but the child died.

The infant was the son of the *sagamore* (chief) Squando, one of the mightiest of Indian leaders, who quickly carried out terrible vengeance on the settlers. This was said to be one of the final events which led to a period of eighty-five years of warfare with the Indians in Maine. Most of New England was involved as King Philip's War shattered the peace of Maine when Saco was attacked on September 18, 1675. Then Scarborough was burned. When Casco was sacked, people were either killed, taken captive, or driven to the outlying islands of the bay. The Indians advanced on Portland in 1676, killing and burning as they came. The colonists made a stand at the foot of High Street. Nevertheless, as one historian wrote: "The doom of Falmouth [then the name of Portland] was pronounced at once. . . . It was crushed by a single blow." Some of the people escaped to Massachusetts, while others fled to Jewell Island.

In 1678, the government of Massachusetts was able to make a treaty with the Indians, providing a short uneasy period of peace. Massachusetts appointed Thomas Danforth as president of Maine in 1680. When the English King took direct command of the New England colonies, he appointed Sir Edmund Andros to consolidate the government of the entire New England region.

Andros attacked Penobscot and sacked the powerful stronghold of French Baron de St. Castin in 1688. This was the beginning in Maine of what is known as King William's War. The first reprisal of the French and Indians came when Indian forces attacked. Andros was removed from his command, but the war with the French and their Indian allies continued. Pemaquid fell in 1689; Newichawannock (now Berwick) in 1690. Baron de St. Castin attacked Falmouth (now Portland) with his force of five hundred Indians and French from

Canada. After a three-day battle, the defenders of Fort Loyal at Falmouth surrendered and were promised safety, but as soon as the doors were opened the French abandoned them to the Indians, and many were killed. Many women and children who survived were taken to Canada as prisoners.

Sir William Phips advanced into Canada. He captured Port Royal but failed to take Quebec. Fort William Henry at Pemaquid had been called "the most expensive and the strongest fortification that had ever been built by the English on American soil." When the French captured it, they had reached the peak of their power in the region and of their influence over the Indians.

When the fall of 1691 arrived, only four towns—York, Wells, Appledore, and Kittery—were still inhabited in all of what is now Maine. Fighting continued, and the French were not always successful. A tiny force of fifteen held off a two-day siege by five hundred French and Indian troops on the Joseph Storer Garrison House near Wells. However, when warfare was suspended by the Treaty of Ryswick in 1697, the French claimed all the territory east of the Penobscot.

What remained came under the administration of the first royal governor, Sir William Phips, in 1691. Under his guidance Maine began a period of real growth. However, this did not continue without interruption. With their numbers reduced by war and epidemic, the Indians made a last desperate effort to save their lands, combining again with the French in what was called Queen Anne's War. It began in 1703 and lasted for ten years. When the war ended in 1713, much of the Indians' power and influence had vanished forever.

A period of expansion and prosperity began which continued for several years. By 1743 the population had grown to twelve thousand. However, yet another war broke out in 1744, and a year later Damariscotta and Fort St. George were attacked. The last of the Indian wars was known in the colonies as the French and Indian War. The French were driven from the North American continent in 1763, but peace came to the Maine region as early as 1760, when a treaty was signed in April with the scattered remaining Indian tribes near Fort Pownal.

28

In eighty-five years of warfare, more than a thousand Maine residents had been killed and hundreds captured.

THEIR MAINE INTEREST WAS FREEDOM

As in the other colonies, the people of Maine had become increasingly irritated by British rule. They were particularly angry at the rule which gave the best trees in Maine to the king's navy because the trunks made the world's finest masts. Navy representatives had first choice of all trees, and the royal mark on these trees caused many to turn against the king. Maine in 1765 joined the other colonies in protesting the taxes assessed by the British Parliament.

Delegates at a 1774 convention in Falmouth declared a "firm and persevering opposition to every design, dark or open, framed to abridge our English liberties." In 1775 the Continental Congress formed the district of Maine. Some of the most interesting early events of the American Revolution took place at the little town of Machias and at Machiasport.

Machias had been requested to supply lumber for British troop barracks. The townspeople gathered on the banks of a little stream to discuss the matter. Finally, Benjamin Foster, a local rebel leader, jumped across the stream and asked those who were with him to follow him across. Practically everyone followed his lead, and the community was committed to the Revolution. The stream has come to be known as Foster's Rubicon, because there Foster forced a decision just as Julius Caesar had done so long before when he crossed the Rubicon River.

When the British sent the armed schooner *Margaretta* to Machiasport to bring back the lumber in convoy, the townspeople, led by Foster and Jeremiah O'Brien, commandeered two boats, captured the *Margaretta,* and killed its commander. This small engagement, which took place five days before the battle of Bunker Hill, has been called "the first naval battle of the Revolution." It also has become known as the "Lexington of the seas," comparing it to the first land fighting in the Revolution.

Henry Knox hauled 59 dismantled cannon from Fort Ticonderoga over 300 tortuous miles of mountains for the siege of Boston, painting by Tom Lovell.

Maine was the scene of many hardships during one of the country's strangest and most ill-fated military expeditions. Some American leaders believed that Canada might join the Revolution if a major Canadian city could be captured. Two separate military forces were sent north to take Quebec. One of these, consisting of eleven hundred men, was led by Benedict Arnold, then still loyal to the American cause.

In September 1775, Arnold's force reached the Kennebec River.

The party was delayed because boats had to be made for the shallower parts of the rivers; the autumn rains came, and many men became ill. At Eustis, the Arnold force went up the Dead River, where several scows loaded with provisions were sunk and many undisciplined men turned back.

The group finally reached Canada and met the force led by General Richard Montgomery, but Arnold had only 510 men left and Montgomery 500. Although they managed to enter Quebec, they were driven out, with Montgomery killed and Arnold wounded.

The cities and towns of Maine suffered more in the Revolution than most of the other New England areas. In October 1775 a fleet of British ships arrived at Falmouth and demanded that the people give up all their arms. When they bravely refused, the commander, Captain Henry Mowatt, ordered the town evacuated. His fleet opened fire and pounded the community for a day and a night. The buildings that had escaped bombardment were burned.

More than four hundred buildings were destroyed, including a new courthouse, and two thousand people were made homeless. The only public building not destroyed was the Widow Grele's tavern. Whenever it began to burn, the courageous woman hurried out with pails of water and put out the fire.

Almost every coastal town felt the British wrath. The king's forces occupied and commanded the Penobscot region, and thirty-three ships were destroyed in the Penobscot River alone. However, the inability of the British to get Maine masts out of the country seriously crippled the British navy, since no other masts were nearly as suitable.

During the war, Maine men were often in significant roles. More than a thousand from Maine suffered through the awful hardships of Valley Forge. The long hard years of the French and Indian wars had provided much invaluable military experience, and many Maine residents rose to high rank and other leadership positions during the American Revolution.

At last the weary days of the war were over; a new nation was formed, and the colonies became states, except for Maine, which remained a division of Massachusetts.

Yesterday and Today

In 1790 the first United States census showed Maine with a population of 96,540.

The first of several disputes with the British over the boundary line with Canada was settled in 1815. Both sides agreed that the River St. Croix was to be the point from which the eastern boundary line would be drawn, but each side claimed a different river was the St. Croix. An old map of Champlain's and an examination of the ruins of the old du Guast settlement on Dochet Island helped to decide the matter in the United States' favor. Otherwise, much of what is now eastern Maine might be in Canada today.

In spite of this settlement, other difficulties with Britain continued. Maine's shipping and commerce both were adversely affected when the United States placed an embargo on British shipments in 1807. In attempting to get around this embargo, Eastport was used for large-scale smuggling from Canada, and it became a thriving center of that illegal enterprise.

The difficulties with Britain grew and once more led to war. Because of Maine's importance in shipping and shipbuilding, once again it suffered greatly in wartime. The British seized the land as far west as the Penobscot and declared the territory to be a province of New Brunswick.

Major ports, shipyards and other installations were major targets for British raiders in other parts of Maine. In September 1814, a defenseless Bangor was captured by British army and navy forces, made to surrender unconditionally, and forced to pay tribute.

Not all the victories in the northern regions went to Britain. The brig *American Enterprise* captured the British brig *Boxer* in a battle between Seguin and Monhegan. Commanders of both vessels were killed; the captured British ship and the bodies of the commanders—American Lieutenant William Burrows and British Captain Samuel Blyth—were brought to Portland. The two brave young officers' bodies were rowed ashore in a ten-oared barge, followed by most of

Opposite: Stonington, Maine.

33

the boats in the harbor as guns boomed in tribute. Masters of the various ships manned the oars of the funeral barge. Burrows and Blyth are buried side by side in Portland's old Eastern Cemetery. Congress later struck a commemorative medal to honor Burrows.

In his poem "My Lost Youth," Longfellow described the event:

> I remember the sea fight far away,
> How it thundered o'er the tide!
> And the dead captains, as they lay
> In their graves, o'erlooking the tranquil bay
> Where they in battle died.

When the war ended, the treaty of 1814 left Maine's boundaries exactly as they were before the war. The last British troops left their captured Maine territory in 1815. A joint commission settled the question of ownership of islands in Passamaquoddy Bay. The United States was allotted Dudley, Frederick, and Moose islands.

THE STATE OF MAINE

For almost two hundred years Maine, as the district of Maine, had been a part of Massachusetts. However, as someone has said, it would be more fitting to think of Maine as an "older sister" of Massachusetts rather than a "daughter." The first Massachusetts settlers were welcomed by Samoset in English which he had learned in Maine. Maine fishermen and Indians provided the food and supplies needed by the Plymouth colony, and the province of Maine was officially named before Massachusetts.

Massachusetts had failed to defend Maine during the War of 1812, and the Bay State was considered unfair to Maine in many matters, particularly in education. There was also the theory that government would be better and cheaper if carried on at a lesser distance. At various times in the past, there had been much agitation for separation. Finally, in 1819, Maine broke away from Massachusetts. Freeport claims the title of Birthplace of Maine because the final

Passamaquoddy Bay and Pulpit Rock.

papers separating Maine from Massachusetts were signed there by commissioners of both states. On March 15, 1820, Maine was admitted as a full-fledged state—the twenty-third in the Union. At that time Maine boasted of 236 incorporated towns. Portland was named the capital, and William King was elected the first state governor.

In 1827, Augusta was chosen the capital, and the cornerstone was laid for the capitol building in 1829. The seat of government was moved from Portland to Augusta in 1832.

The never-ending argument about the boundary between Maine and Canada continued after statehood. The king of the Netherlands was accepted by both sides in 1831 to arbitrate the dispute. He recommended a compromise boundary line in which the British would relinquish more of their claim than the Americans; nevertheless, the British accepted this. However, Maine protested so vigorously that the United States Senate would not accept the king's award.

As the years went on, the disagreement grew more bitter. Several forts, including Fort Knox, the Gibraltar of the Penobscot, were constructed for defending the area. Maine mobilized its militia. In 1839 Maine militiamen tramped 200 miles (322 kilometers) across wilderness and deep snow to drive out Canadian lumbermen who were working in a region claimed by Maine. Many border clashes occurred in what came to be known as the Aroostook War. Congress authorized the president to raise fifty thousand troops, and it looked as if real warfare might break out.

At this point, Daniel Webster, then U. S. secretary of state, made one of his many great contributions to his country. Lord Ashburton, who represented Great Britain, had been given a map that was made for King George III, which he felt weakened the British position. On

Fort Knox was built to protect Maine from Canadian attack.

the other hand, Webster had a map marked by Benjamin Franklin which he felt weakened his position.

Neither man knew of the other's map, but, possibly feeling their lack of strength, both men negotiated with a friendly calm which set a new tone in British-American relations. The result was the Webster-Ashburton Treaty of 1842, establishing once and for all the Maine-Canada border. The border between the United States and Canada has endured since that time as the world's longest undefended boundary between nations.

Strangely, Maine lost in the Webster-Ashburton Treaty about 5,500 square miles (14,245 square kilometers) that might have been part of the state if it had been willing to accept the offer of the king of the Netherlands eleven years before.

NORTH AGAINST SOUTH

The second quarter of the nineteenth century saw many causes and crusades in Maine. The liquor trade, the Masonic order, Catholicism and Catholic clerics, and slavery were all assailed. Most of these attacks diminished in intensity, but the antislavery campaign grew.

Few blacks had ever been held as slaves in Maine. Nevertheless, the inhumanity of slaveholding in other states resulted in the formation of an antislavery society in Maine as early as 1833, and a statewide society was formed the next year. By 1841 every county had an antislavery society, and the groups ran a candidate for governor of Maine.

The coastal towns, which had strong commercial ties with the South, were generally opposed to the antislavery or abolitionist movement. However, most of the interior was violently opposed to slavery. In 1857, the first year that the new Republican party had statewide candidates for office, their candidate Hannibal Hamlin was elected governor of Maine on a platform vigorously opposing slavery.

When President Abraham Lincoln called for volunteers to serve during the Civil War, Maine hurried to respond, although the state government was unprepared for war. Huge public meetings were held to pledge support of the federal government.

During the war, Maine's commerce suffered greatly from the actions of the Confederate navy, and home guards were organized to repel coastal attacks. One dramatic incident occurred when a small Confederate force of sailors disguised themselves as fishermen and slipped into the harbor of Portland.

There they took the revenue cutter *Caleb Cushing* and sailed away. When the act was discovered, the mayor of Portland and the customs chief took off in pursuit in boats with volunteer crews. They recaptured the *Cushing* and took the Confederate crew captive after they had set fire to the cutter.

Altogether, about sixty-seven thousand Maine men served in the Civil War, and eighty-eight hundred of these lost their lives. Portland had the incredible record of providing fully a fifth of its total population for Civil War service. Generals O.O. Howard, a hero of Gettysburg, and Joshua L. Chamberlain were among the Civil War leaders from Maine.

Recruits from Maine were known for their bravery and vigor, which was due probably to the rugged outdoor lives so many of them had led. Deer running was one activity that kept many Maine men in shape. When a deer is shot, it often has the strength to dash across the woods and fields for miles, with the hunter running hard behind. A popular Civil War story concerned the young Maine soldier, an experienced deer runner, who was left on sentry duty. When the others retreated in the face of a Confederate advance, he found himself alone facing the enemy. He set out running with such speed that he made the nineteen miles (thirty kilometers) from Cedar Creek to Harpers Ferry before the dispatch bearer arrived on horseback.

The great shipyards of Maine were particularly important to the Union in providing support for the American navy. One of the best-known ships of the Civil War was the *Kearsarge*, built at the Kittery yards. In one of the war's major battles, the *Kearsarge*, under Captain John A. Winslow, defeated and sank the famed Confederate raider *Alabama*.

38

A MODERN STATE

Escaping destruction during the Civil War, Portland was not so fortunate after the war ended. In 1866 the city was almost wiped out by a fire that began on the Fourth of July. A strong south wind carried the flames across much of the city. Only the blowing up of many buildings to clear the path of the fire saved the remainder of the city. The poet Longfellow wrote: "I have been in Portland since the fire. Desolation, desolation, desolation! It reminds me of Pompeii."

Fortunately, no one was killed, and tent cities began to spring up to house the homeless. The city started immediately to rebuild; in many areas better planning than in prefire days was utilized.

The years that followed were a period of great change and expansion in manufacturing, commerce, transportation, and other important areas. These are covered more fully in later sections. The state suffered many hardships in the nationwide depression of the 1890s.

At the outbreak of World War I, the German liner *Kronprinzessin Cecilie* was anchored in Bar Harbor. When it was taken and held in port, the liner was found to be carrying a cargo of gold.

During the war Maine provided more than 35,000 service men and women. Of these, 1,073 lost their lives. One of Maine's wartime heroes was Charles Nola, a Passamaquoddy Indian. For his remarkable bravery and stubborn courage in defending an advance post until he died, he was awarded, posthumously, the Croix de Guerre of France.

One of the many ways in which Maine helped in the war effort was the shipping of most of Canada's wheat and other grain through the port of Portland.

In 1924 Maine had a part in one of the exciting episodes of the time. On the first round-the-world flight, made by United States Army pilots, the first United States soil touched after the trailblazing trip was Mere Point, near Brunswick. The next year the famed Mac-Millan Arctic expedition sailed from Wiscasset.

For centuries men have dreamed of harnessing and using the immense power of the tides as they sweep in and out from the world's oceans. One of the favorite locations for such a project has always been Passamaquoddy Bay, where the country's greatest tides dramatically rise and fall. Work on the Passamaquoddy Tidal Power Project was begun in 1935, then abandoned in 1936. Although this project is still little more than a dream, it remains one of the fond hopes of many engineers and planners. In an age of engineering miracles and alternate energy sources, it is not unlikely that someday the wave power of Passamaquoddy Bay will yet flow through the nation's electric lines.

During World War II, more than 95,000 men and women of Maine served in the armed forces. Once again, the state's shipbuilding industry played an important part in providing armaments of war.

Maine also attracted national attention by electing an independent governor in 1974, for the first time in modern history.

By the late 1970s one of the most interesting concerns in Maine was the willingness of the courts to consider the Indian claims for large areas of the state that had been taken away by illegal treaties.

THE PEOPLE OF MAINE

Maine is a state of friendly people, and few states can boast more rugged individualists. People are recognized for individual merit. Many craftsmen are persons of consequence in their own communities, along with the more wealthy and influential persons. The effect of the sea is a strong one on Maine's people. Many of the coastal people have the personality and character usually connected with long association with the sea.

One of the largest ethnic groups in Maine is the French-Canadians. There are at least 150,000 in the state at the present time, especially in northern Maine. Even in the south, Biddeford is 62 percent French-American, and most people speak both French and English. A monthly bilingual journal is published at the University of Maine.

Waterville has a large number of people of Syrian background. Scandinavians, Poles, Russians, Italians, Portuguese, Greeks, and blacks are all an honored part of the Maine scene today.

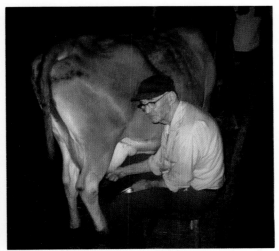

Top left: Indians in traditional dress.
Bottom left: Mr. Kennedy milking.
Top right: Tractor pull contest.
Bottom right: Youngsters bob for apples.

About four thousand Indians remain in Maine. Treaties established the Penobscot and Passamaquoddy tribes as "nations" within the state and gave them certain lands. The Penobscot reservation is at Indian Island (Old Town). The Passamaquoddy are at Pleasant Point (Eastport) and Indian Township (Princeton). The Indians still have income from various agreements and property rights. They are citizens of the United States, but they cannot become citizens of the state without giving up their treaty rights as nations.

Each Indian village elects its own local government, headed by a chief. The elected chief is called governor. Penobscot people have kept their skills in basketmaking, sewing, and pattern work.

Natural Treasures

MIGHTY MONARCHS

On its official state shield, Maine has honored two of its mightiest monarchs—the stately bull moose and the lofty white pine, also selected as the state tree. An early traveler wrote that the pine trees were so tall that "the clouds were torn as they passed over them."

When Europeans first visited what is now Maine, they found practically all of the land covered with forests, and lumbering began almost at once. The philosopher Henry David Thoreau called lumbering a "war against the pines."

Maine was the first state to be concerned with forest conservation. As early as 1656 the first order was issued in Maine against the waste of timber, and Maine was the first state to build forest lookout towers to guard against the ravages of fire. In 1921 Maine was the first to hire a trained entomologist, one who studies insects, for scientific assistance in forest management. Until 1972, unorganized townships in Maine were governed by Forestry District governors.

After more than three hundred years of use to the people, the Maine forests still cover 87 percent of the state nearly 18 million acres (7.2 million hectares).

The white pine provides the nickname Pine Tree State for Maine. The tallest of these trees reach 240 feet (73 meters) in height, and some have been 6 feet (1.8 meters) across at the base. Hemlock, with its bark used for tanning; balsam fir, most valuable for paper pulp; red spruce; white spruce; white cedar; and pitch pine are other trees of the evergreen type.

White, or paper, birch is widespread and valuable. Yellow birch, sugar maple (brilliantly colored in the fall), tamarack, American willow, aspen, poplar, beech, and ironwood are plentiful. Thought to be the oldest trees in Maine and among the most valuable are the white oaks.

Opposite: Moose at Baxter State Park.

One of the rarest of trees is the prostrate savin, or trailing yew, found on Monhegan Island.

FINNY TREASURES

Probably no resource of Maine is better known than the multitude and variety of fish and other marine life. Maine lies adjacent to 200,000 square miles (518,000 square kilometers) of one of the world's finest fishing territories, containing thirty-eight edible kinds of fish. To this, thousands of fishing streams and lakes teeming with trout and salmon and other fish must be added.

Maine has the only Atlantic salmon rivers in the nation. Even more famous are the landlocked salmon. These salmon spend their

Maine is well known for its excellent lobsters.

lives in fresh water without migrating to salt water. These unusual fish are thought to have originated in Sebago Lake and its tributaries, and Maine still has a virtual monopoly on this rare breed. More than ninety lakes and rivers have been stocked with this fisherman's prize. Other popular inland fish include trout—brook, brown, rainbow, and lake—black bass, white perch, and pickerel.

Waters of the Maine coast provide excellent sport fishing. Bluefin tuna, tautog, swordfish, mackerel, sand and winter flounder, cunner, cod, cusk, and haddock rank high in the favor of sport fishermen.

Finback whales may be spotted off the coast, and clams, crabs, shrimp, scallops, and mussels are plentiful. These are all overshadowed, of course, by the famous Maine lobster, about which more will be said later.

ON FOOT, CLAW, AND FLIPPER

In spite of the enormous amount of hunting done during the history of Maine, the total population of game animals is increasing. The most popular game animal—deer—is reaching record numbers. Each year about forty thousand deer are taken. Theodore Roosevelt called the Maine deer the "outstanding specimen of their kind in the world."

The sustained bellow of the bull moose may still be heard in the Maine woods. Occasionally one may be seen calmly and majestically grazing by the roadside. They are protected in Maine; hunting them is illegal.

Maine has the second largest number of bears of any state in the nation, and they may be hunted during seven months of the year. Red fox, bobcats, raccoon, and rabbits are also popular with Maine hunters.

Beaver, once the most hunted of all Maine animals, are now increasing in numbers. However, the packs of wolves that once followed the stagecoaches and could be heard howling mournfully in the deep woods have disappeared. The Maine weasel is the only

The black-capped chickadee is the state bird of Maine.

animal to have taken the name of the state. One of the most interesting of Maine's animals is aquatic—the popular and plentiful seal.

Maine has chosen the chickadee as its state bird. It is probable that the chickadee's qualities as a good neighbor—optimistic, industrious, sociable, and self-confident—appealed to the people of the state, who are known for similar characteristics.

More than three hundred species of birds have been spotted within the state's boundaries. Bird life is particularly interesting in Baxter State Park, which has birds not generally seen in other parts of the state. Unusual shore birds include the razor-billed auk, laughing gull, and puffin or sea parrot. The Cranberry Islands are another location for birds not normally seen in these regions. One of these is Leach's petrel, usually found only far out at sea, which lays its eggs on the islands. Puffins are found on Matinicus Rock, their southernmost nesting point.

Maine is a paradise for the bird hunter. The ruffed grouse, or partridge, is known as "king of Maine upland game birds." Woodcock, nicknamed "timber doodle," pheasants, and ducks are among the other popular game birds. Maine's duck hunting is particularly outstanding, with hundreds of miles of coast and thousands of inland lakes and streams providing numerous sites. Merry-meeting Bay, at the mouth of the Kennebec River, is one of the most famous duck hunting grounds in the East.

46

People Use Their Treasures

HEIRS OF THE BROAD ARROW—FOREST PRODUCTS

When the king's representative marked one of Maine's lofty white pines with a "broad arrow," from that moment on it became "sacred" as a future mast for the Royal Navy. Only the navy could use it; many timber owners, enraged at this violation of their property rights, harvested the broad-arrow trees and defied the law. Local judges were so sympathetic to them that few were ever convicted for illegal use of the prized broad-arrow trees.

The great value placed on these trees is typical of the esteem in which the world has always held Maine's forest products. Maine's principal industry for more than three hundred years has been the harvesting and manufacturing of trees into useful products. In early days, shingles and other wood items were used as currency in Maine. By 1830 Maine led all states in timber production. The peak year of Maine lumber production was 1909. Although no longer first among the states in wood products, the annual value of finished wood products in Maine is impressive.

Lumbering in Maine was helped by the great number of rivers down which the logs could be sent to the sea for processing or shipment. Still vivid is the scene of the great logs roaring down such rivers as the Kennebec, plunging over the crest of Taconic Falls after a hectic dash down the Five Mile Rips north of Waterville, in the picturesque days of the river log drives. River logging like this is now illegal in the state.

Maine has been a pioneer in many fields of the lumber business. The first sawmill in the United States was built at York in 1623. At one time there were 160 sawmills on the Kennebec River alone. Less than fifty years after construction of the first mill, the first "gang" sawmill in North America was built at Great Works. Between 1914 and 1930, Maine led all the states in production of wood pulp. Pulp and paper production is still the principal part of Maine's timber-based industry. The largest newsprint producer in the country is located in Maine.

Lobsterman checks his traps in Stonington, Maine.

HARVESTING THE SEA

To many people, the words Maine and lobster are almost synonymous. A popular site of Maine's lobster industry is Monhegan Island, where lobsters are protected and may be trapped only from January 1 through June 25. Lobster pots, looking like chicken crates, are made of oak lath. The bait inside attracts lobsters, which can enter easily but cannot get out because of the funnel-shaped nets on the entrance. Trap tenders go out to sea in all but the most extreme weather. The largest lobster ever caught was a thirty-six-pound (sixteen-kilogram) monster captured in Casco Bay. Many Maine restaurants are famous for their lobster "pounds," where live lobsters are selected by the customers and then cooked in seaweed.

More than half of Maine's commercial fishing income comes from lobsters—17,000,000 pounds (7,711,064 kilograms), valued at $30 million annually. Total income of the nine thousand commercial fishermen in Maine averages more than $30 million per year. Some of Maine's seafood is shipped fresh by air. Maine processors also operate modern packing plants producing a variety of canned and frozen seafood delicacies that are shipped to all states and many other parts of the world. The herring catch is packed in nearly two million cases a year. Frozen seafood is growing more popular. Even the scales of such fish as herring are used to make an iridescent paint solution.

The Maine country, of course, was pioneered by fishermen, and settlers came later. The fisherman's life in Maine has never been easy. As early as 1623, Christopher Levett was driven to refute the claims of the easy life in Maine, when he wrote: "Nor will the deare come when they are called, or stand still and looke on a man untill he shute him . . . nor the fish leape into the kettle. But certainly there is fowle, Deare, and Fish enough for the taking if men be diligent." The men of Maine have indeed been diligent, even down to the present time, especially in the matter of harvesting the sea.

DOWN TO THE SEA GO THE SHIPS

Christopher Levett observed in Maine that ships could be "as conveniently built there as in any place in the world, where I have beene, and better cheape." This was borne out when, only twenty-four years after the *Virginia* was built, John Winter, a pioneer American shipbuilder, established a shipyard on Richmond Island. His vessels carried lumber, fish, oil, and other products to England.

Ever since that time, Maine has been a leader in shipbuilding. By 1812 a third of all registered American ship tonnage had been built in Maine.

Bath has been Maine's leading shipbuilding center almost since the construction of the first ship. During this period, more than four thousand ships totalling close to 2,000,000 tons (1,814,370 metric tons) have been launched into the Kennebec River there. The world's first steel sailing vessel (a four-master) was made at Bath. The Bath Iron Works is still one of the nation's major shipbuilders. During World War II Bath turned out 86 destroyers, and the South Portland yards delivered 274 cargo ships of 10,000 tons (9,072 metric tons) each. Nearly a fourth of all the destroyers built in the United States during that time were Bath-built.

"Hove to for a Pilot" by Currier & Ives recalls the great days of the clipper ship.

Today, Bath is in step with the times, building, among many other things guided missile destroyers. In fact, the Bath yards built the first guided missile destroyer.

Although the naval shipyard at Kittery, Maine, is known as the Portsmouth (New Hampshire) Naval Shipyard, it is wholly located in Maine. The Kittery naval shipyard is the largest single industry in the country north of Boston. The first vessel launched there was the *Washington,* in 1815. In 1917 the first navy-constructed submarine was built there. During World War II, seventy-five submarines were built there. On one day, January 27, 1944, four undersea ships were launched. The navy's first atomic submarine, U.S.S. *Swordfish,* was launched at Kittery in 1956. The *Sea Dragon,* also launched at Kittery after its completion in 1959, was the first ship to sail the famed Northwest Passage completely under the ice. Now the Kittery yard also builds the Polaris type atomic missile subs.

In addition to Maine's two major shipbuilding yards, about seventy-five smaller ones produce ships today, and shipbuilding is the principal industry in about fifty coastal and river towns.

Many famous ships have been built in Maine yards. The *Wyoming* was the largest wooden ship afloat in its time; it was known as the "wonder ship." In 1854 the clipper *Red Jacket* set a sailing record from New York to England that has never been broken. The first ship to fly the stars and stripes was John Paul Jones's *Ranger,* made at Kittery. The *Roosevelt,* Admiral Peary's North Pole ship, was built

50

at Verona, and the 1937 America's Cup race winner, *Ranger*, was constructed at Bath.

Two interesting arts have grown up in connection with Maine's preoccupation with shipbuilding. One is the art of figurehead carving. Some of the finest of this work was done in Maine, and many good examples have been preserved in museums throughout the state. Also spurred by shipbuilding was the art of model shipmaking. Many a retired seafaring man or shipbuilder has taken up this demanding craft, and Maine ship models are much in demand.

"I A LIGHT CANOE WILL BUILD ME"—OTHERS MANUFACTURES

From the biggest to the smallest, Maine makes many types of watercraft. The world's largest canoe manufacturer is the Old Town plant. Many descendants of the first canoe builders—the Indians—are skillful workers in the canoe plants.

Maine industries also manage to turn the largest products into the smallest. Each year, Maine's great trees are turned into billions of toothpicks, and the state boasts the world's largest toothpick plant.

One of the unusual products of Maine was ice. Almost as soon as the crystal-clear waters of the state froze, hardy crews swarmed out over the ice with cutters. The ice blocks were stored in great icehouses. Ships leaving Maine would take on ice as ballast and deliver it to warm regions where an ice-cooled drink was in great demand. The first cargo of Maine ice went to Baltimore in 1826. The Maine ice industry flourished from 1840 through the 1890s. In 1890, 3,000,000 tons (2,721,555 metric tons) of Maine ice were shipped.

Another once-flourishing Maine industry was the tanneries. At one time four hundred tanneries operated in Maine, using the plentiful hemlock tanbark. Tanning, leather, footwear, and allied products still make up Maine's fourth largest industry.

Lumber, wood, paper, pulp and allied products each year provide over a third of Maine's manufacturing income. Food products are ranked second, with more than $600 million in value each year; leather products in 1977 accounted for $400 million. Printing, transportation equipment, fabricated metals, textiles, electrical machinery, stone and glass products, and chemicals are other substantial industries in Maine.

Maine has long been noted for its distinctive craft industries. Village carpenters early gained a reputation as "incredibly fine artisans." The technique of hooked rug making is said to have originated in Maine. The designs were original, and wool came from home-raised sheep. The earliest rugs were hooked on hand-loomed linen backing. Dyes came from local coloring materials, such as maple and butternut for dull greens and browns, onion peels for yellows, and beet root for reds.

Portland's famous glass manufacturing industry was founded in 1863.

The total value of Maine's manufactured products at present exceeds $4 billion.

AGRICULTURE—DIG THAT CROP!

It is claimed that something about Maine's soil produces a distinctive flavor in its agricultural products, such as apples and peas. This is especially true of the tantalizing flavor of Maine sweet corn and the robust flavor of Maine potatoes.

No single agricultural crop in Maine is more famous than the potato. Each year Maine grows a sixth of all the white potatoes produced in the United States. They account for about 40 percent of the state's normal farm income.

Aroostook County is regarded as one of the nation's best potato regions. In late summer, when the potatoes blossom, the potato fields are transformed for a short time into flower gardens, with blankets of waving blooms of white, pink, and violet potato blossoms. A total of 140,000 acres (56,656 hectares) is planted in potatoes, and the potato crop is valued at about $200 million per year. Half of the crop is of such superior quality that it is certified by the Maine Seed Potato Board to be sold as seed, and about a fourth of the crop actually is sold for seed purposes. The board operates a

Harvesting potatoes in Aroostook County.

foundation seed farm at Masardis, where a nationally known program is carried on to improve potato stocks.

A comparatively small but notable Maine crop is blueberries. Maine provides 90 percent of all the nation's processed blueberries. The fruit is harvested with dustpan-like rakes. There are more than enough Maine blueberries to provide everyone in the United States with a piece of Maine's marvelous blueberry pie.

Another large income producer in Maine agriculture is poultry. All livestock, including poultry, accounts for an average yearly income of $246 million.

Total agricultural income in the state of Maine is close to $400 million per year.

MINERALS

Although Maine ranks low among the states in mineral production, it has had some notable successes in minerals. The largest emerald beryl ever found came from the Bumpus mine near

53

Lynchville, and there are many other gems and rare minerals found in the state. Maine has one of the world's largest reserves of low-grade manganese iron ore. Twenty-five percent of all the feldspar in the United States is produced in Maine. Considerable use is made of the large peat deposits. Asbestos and diatomaceous earth are also important.

The pink granite of the Penobscot Islands is Maine's most recognized mineral. Maine granite has been used in some of the country's famous structures, including Grant's Tomb, the Philadelphia Mint, and the St. Louis Post Office. Granite from Vinalhaven Island was used in the great Cathedral of St. John the Divine in New York.

Total annual value of Maine mineral products is about $50 million.

TRANSPORTATION, COMMUNICATION, AND POWER

The many harbors and rivers supplied the first avenues for transportation in what John Greenleaf Whittier called "hundred-harbored Maine." Ocean ships have access to ten of the sixteen counties of the state, and there are ten ports of entry. Bangor was once the world's largest timber shipping port. More than seven hundred vessels have been anchored in Bangor harbor at one time. In 1840 a whole fleet of schooners was in operation from Augusta to Boston.

The first steamboat puffed up the Kennebec in 1822, and the first transatlantic steamer reached Portland in 1853. The port of Portland is nineteenth in volume in the United States, handling 15,500,000 tons (14,061,368 metric tons) of shipping a year. The $1,500,000 State Pier at Portland Harbor greatly facilitates the city in keeping its rank as one of the nation's major ports.

Maine's earliest overland routes were trails blazed by the Indians—combinations of waterways and "carries," or portages. The first stagecoach operated in Maine in 1787. By 1816 there was a well-established stagecoach route from New York through Boston to Bangor. Many fascinating stories are told of the hardships and adventure of stage travel in those early days.

Trains have been operating in Maine since 1836.

Today's swift travel over superb modern roads is in sharp contrast to the stagecoach era. The Maine Turnpike from Kittery to Augusta was completed in 1955. Building its 106 scenic, beautifully engineered miles (170 kilometers) was one of the largest single construction projects. Interstate Highway 95 north from Portland to the Canadian border is another important route.

One of the United States' most historic highways begins in Maine. U. S. Route 1 starts near Fort Kent on the Canadian border and stretches down the whole eastern coastline of the country to its end at Key West, Florida.

The first railroad in Maine, one of the earliest in the United States, began to operate from Bangor to Old Town in 1836.

In 1845 one of America's most unusual races decided the location of the winter terminus of a Canadian railway. Both Portland, Maine, and Boston, Massachusetts, wanted the honor. A ship from England brought two special mailbags—one for each city. Whichever city's representative reached Montreal first with its mailbag would win the terminus.

Portland sent a tug out to meet the steamer. Every seven miles (eleven kilometers) between Portland and Montreal, fresh relays of horses had been arranged to pull the mail sleigh over the New England snows. Just outside of Montreal a special team and one of the largest drivers to be found (named Grosvenor Waterhouse) took over the mailbag. With the American flag fluttering from the whip-socket, the mail sleigh and its imposing driver dashed proudly into the Canadian city in a last great burst of rapidity. The 255 miles (410 kilometers) had been covered in eighteen hours and six minutes. This beat the Boston mail by several hours, and Portland became the terminus. Today, Portland is still the winter terminus of the mammoth Canadian National Railroad, when the St. Lawrence River is frozen over.

Maine's first newspaper was the *Falmouth Gazette,* founded in 1875. The first daily newspaper in the state, the *Portland Courier,* was begun in 1829. The *Portland Press-Herald* has the state's largest daily circulation.

The beauties and attractions of Maine are responsible for one of its biggest industries—tourism. In all seasons, visitors find Maine irresistible for vacation pleasure, for scenery, sport, and just plain relaxation. Annual tourist expenditures exceed $350 million.

Almost from the beginning, waterpower has had tremendous importance in Maine, where water-powered corn grinding mills were the first of their kind in New England. Today, the rivers are held by large numbers of dams so that they are now almost completely controlled, and property damage from floods is rare. Considerably more than half the power produced in Maine is hydroelectric. However, less than a fourth of the possible hydroelectric power of Maine has yet been developed. An estimated 1,600,000 kilowatts of waterpower still remains untapped in Maine.

56

Human Treasures

A CORNER ON POETRY

Only one American poet has ever been admitted to the Poet's Corner of England's Westminster Abbey, and that was Maine native Henry Wadsworth Longfellow. Maine, in fact, can claim to have been the birthplace of more great American poets than any other state. It has been said that within a 100-mile (161-kilometer) radius of the state capitol, there are more literary landmarks than in any similar area in the country.

Longfellow was born in 1807 in "the beautiful town that is seated by the sea," as he later wrote of Portland. His noted birthplace, his aunt's home, is famous in its own right as the first brick building erected in Portland. This was built by his well-known grandfather, General Peleg Wadsworth.

The future poet grew up in Maine; the budding genius started school at the age of three. He rode to school behind a servant on the broad back of a family horse. He enrolled at Bowdoin College when he was only fourteen. He studied in several European countries and became skilled in many languages. Later, Longfellow was appointed a professor and librarian at Bowdoin. His first book of poetry, *Voices*

Longfellow Monument.

of the Night, was published in 1839, after he had left Bowdoin to become a professor at Harvard.

Longfellow drew the inspiration for many of his poems from his native state. His famous poem "The Wreck of the Hesperus" is based on the disaster that caught the schooner *Eliza* in the great gale of 1869 at Peak's Island. Only one crew member escaped—a boy who had been the only survivor of another wreck, in the West Indies. He decided to live on land where it was safe, but with bitter irony, he fell from a log over a small stream and drowned.

Another Maine incident immortalized by Longfellow was the desperate day-long fight of Captain John Lovewell and his force of thirty-three men against a company of eighty Pequawket Indians led by Sagamore Paugus. Both the captain and chief were killed in the battle, which forced the Pequawket to leave their headquarters, called Pequawket, and flee to Canada. Longfellow's work "My Lost Youth" is based on his experiences in Maine.

Ballads and Other Poems, published by Longfellow in 1841, contained some of his best-known works: "The Village Blacksmith," "Excelsior," and "The Wreck of the Hesperus." *Hiawatha,* the great epic poem and one of the most quoted works in English, appeared in 1855. *The Courtship of Miles Standish* was published in 1858. *Tales of a Wayside Inn,* which contains "Paul Revere's Ride," was completed in 1863. He translated Dante's *Divine Comedy* in three volumes from 1865 to 1867.

When Henry Wadsworth Longfellow died in 1882, he was probably America's best-known and most popular poet. The International Longfellow Society maintained its headquarters in his birthplace, but the society has now disbanded. In later years there has been a tendency to discount the place of Longfellow in American poetry, but he still holds a large place in the history of literature.

OTHER POETIC VOICES

Another Maine-born poet also is probably less popular today than he should be. This is Edwin Arlington Robinson, born at Head Tide in 1869. There are those who feel that Robinson is the greatest American-born poet, but both during his lifetime and after his death in 1935 Edwin Arlington Robinson never received anything like the public recognition so many say he deserved. However, many experts in poetry recognized his merit. Among other honors, he received the Pulitzer Prize for poetry in 1922, 1925, and 1928.

Robinson's early poems were written in and about Maine. He grew up in Gardiner, which is most likely the place he called "Tilbury Town" in his poetry.

Still another major Maine poet is Edna St. Vincent Millay. She was the first American woman to receive the Pulitzer Prize for poetry. Her birthplace was Rockland, where she was born in 1892, and she spent much of her later life in the rugged islands of Casco Bay. Her first long poem, *Renascence,* was published when she was only nine-teen years old. Some critics have called Edna St. Vincent Millay "the greatest woman poet of America."

Yet another major Maine poet, winner of the Pulitzer Prize in 1936, is Robert P. Tristram Coffin. Like Longfellow, Coffin served as a Bowdoin professor. Most of his work uses his native state as a background, about which he wrote:

> This is my country, bitter as the sea,
> Pungent with the fir and bayberry.

One day a Colby College professor of modern languages was glancing through a book of German songs. He liked one of the melodies and decided to write new English words for it. This became the beloved anthem "America" (or "My Country 'Tis of Thee," as it is popularly known), which many believe should have been chosen as our national anthem. The professor, Samuel Francis Smith, also was a minister of the First Baptist Church of Waterville.

Nathaniel Parker Willis, Jr., was well known as a poet. He came from a literary family; his father was the founder of *The Youth's Companion* and *American Monthly Magazine,* and his sister was an in-fluential writer on social causes. MacDonald ("The Mad Poet") Clarke was a poet of considerable reputation and might have gone on to much recognition, but he died in the asylum on New York's Blackwell Island, drowning in the flood from an open faucet.

OTHER CREATIVE SPIRITS

Nathaniel Hawthorne was not a native of Maine, but he spent his boyhood at Raymond in a house near Dingley Brook. Maine is well known for the local storytellers who once gathered around the stove in village general stores. Impressionable young Hawthorne often sat in Manning's store to listen to the wonderful tales, and many incidents in his writing came from the careful notes he kept even at that early age.

One entry in his diary reads: "A peddler named Dominicus Jordan was today in Uncle Richard's store telling a ghost story. I listened intently but tried not to seem interested. The story was of a house, the owner of which was suddenly killed. Since his death the west garret window cannot be kept closed, though the shutters be hasped and nailed at night; they are invariably found open the next morning, and no one can tell when and how the nails were drawn." The peddler Dominicus Jordan appears as Dominicus Pike in the Hawthorne story "Mr. Higginbotham's Castastrophe."

Hawthorne graduated from Bowdoin College in Brunswick, a classmate and friend of Longfellow. His first novel, *Fanshaw,* was a romance of Bowdoin and Brunswick.

Maine has had a number of notable women writers. One of America's first novelists was Sally Sayward Barrell, who wrote under the pen name of Madam Wood. She was born in York in 1759 and was determined to create an American style of writing, based on American scenes and characters. "Why," she wrote, "should we not aim at independence with respect to our mental enjoyments?... Why must the amusements of our leisure hours cross the Atlantic? and introduce foreign fashions and foreign manners to a people certainly capable of producing their own?"

Introducing a novel, she wrote: "The following pages are wholly American; the characters are those of our own country. The author

has endeavored to catch the manners of her native land. . . . "
However, the story is told that when Madam Wood read some of Sir
Walter Scott's novels, she was so unhappy with her own work that
she gathered up as many books and manuscripts as she could and
destroyed them. She lived to be ninety-five years old.

Kate Douglas Wiggin, one of the most popular authors of an earlier day, was born in Buxton Town. Her best-known work is probably
Rebecca of Sunnybrook Farm. Blue Hill was the birthplace of Mary
Ellen Chase, author of *A Goodly Heritage;* this book and her *Mary
Peters* both use her Maine birthplace as settings. Sarah Orne Jewett
was born at South Berwick. She has been called "America's greatest
woman prose writer." She lived most of her life in the Berwick
region, and much of her work concerned it. Her first story was published in *Atlantic Monthly* when she was only twenty.

One of the most famous novels of all time — *Uncle Tom's Cabin* —
was written in Maine. Harriet Beecher Stowe's husband was preaching in Brunswick when Mrs. Stowe wrote the world-renowned book.
Many other writers and artists have worked in Maine, which is particularly favored by creative people as a summer home.

Two of the most successful writers of series books were Maine
natives. Gilbert Patten was born in Newport. Under the pen name of
Bert L. Standish he wrote the "Frank Merriwell" series. These
books at one time were known to almost every boy in the country.

Jacob Abbott has been called "Maine's most prolific writer." He
produced two hundred books for young people. Among the best-known of his works was the "Little Rollo" series.

Two famed American humorists were Maine natives. Edgar
Wilson (Bill) Nye was born at Shirley in 1850; Charles Farrar
Browne, born in 1834 at Waterford in Oxford County, gained fame
as the humorist known as Artemus Ward.

One of the most notable writers of historical novels is Kenneth
Roberts, born at Kennebunk.

The naturalist and writer Henry David Thoreau spent much time
in Maine, and one of his best-known works is "The Maine Woods."

Among Maine's unusual artists was the talented Indian Paul
Orson, whose colors were made from berry juices; he used animal

tails for brushes. His best-known work is *Picture of the Crucifixion* in the church on Indian Island.

Winslow Homer, sometimes called a "foremost figure in American art," lived in Maine from 1884 until his death in 1910. Another prominent art figure who did much to popularize the merit of Maine as a home for the arts was noted illustrator Rockwell Kent. One of the best-known native Maine artists was Atherton Furlong, born in Locke's Mills. Some of his works hang in New York's Metropolitan Museum of Art. Furlong also gained fame as a lyric tenor and teacher of Lillian Nordica.

Lillian Nordica was born in Farmington in 1859. Her older sister was to have been the musical talent of the family, but she died suddenly, and at age fifteen Lillian went secretly to study in the hope that she could achieve her parents' goal of a famous singer in the family. After many difficulties in gaining recognition in competition with foreign singers, she finally attained great fame, and is probably one of the most renowned vocalists ever produced in America.

Lillian Nordica was one of the first performers to have great publicity given to her personal life. One widely publicized incident occurred when she filed to divorce her first husband. He took off on a balloon flight and was never seen again. Even her death was newsworthy. Lillian Nordica died in 1914 on the remote island of Java as a result of exposure when her ship was wrecked off Thursday Island.

John Knowles Paine, called "America's earliest noted composer," was born in Portland in 1839. The error that he was born in the same house as the poet Longfellow has become widespread. This misunderstanding probably came about because a fine doorway from the Paine birthplace was moved to the Longfellow house as a replacement.

Robert B. Hall, born at Bowdoinham, was another of Maine's most prominent musicians. He gained fame as a composer of more than seventy-five marches, some of which are still popular today.

John Neal, a well-known Portland lawyer, poet, and athlete, had an unusual "career" in the arts as an "apostle of American art in London," as he liked to style himself. He said he established himself in London for the sole purpose of demonstrating to Europeans that

America had created a culture of its own. Returning to Portland, he influenced and helped many young American artists.

PUBLIC FIGURES

James G. Blaine, a resident of Augusta, was Maine's only candidate for the presidency of the United States. He served as U.S. Secretary of State in 1881 and became the Republican candidate for president in 1884, losing to Grover Cleveland. In 1889 he again became Secretary of State. He was a noted Speaker of the House of Representatives from 1869 to 1875 and a United States senator.

Hannibal Hamlin is often named as one of Maine's most distinguished citizens. He served as governor of the state and then became vice president of the United States under Lincoln. Hamlin went to the United States Senate in 1869 and served there until 1881. After leaving the Senate, he was minister to Spain until 1883. Hamlin was born in Paris Hill.

Melville W. Fuller, another native of Augusta, served as Chief Justice of the United States for twenty-two years, from 1888 to 1910. During his term, he wrote 829 decisions.

One of the most influential men of his time in politics was Thomas Brackett Reed of Portland, who grew up as one of the Brackett Street Boys in a humble neighborhood of the city. He went to Congress in 1876 and was a member of the House for twenty-two years. As Speaker of the House for three terms, it was said that he "ruled" the House; this gave him his nickname of "Czar" Reed. It is acknowledged that a majority of the present rules of the House came about under his leadership. He was known for his sometimes bitter wit. At one time when a congressman said, "I would rather be right than president," Speaker Reed shot back, "The gentleman from Illinois will never be either."

Reed wanted the Republican presidential nomination in 1900, but lost to William McKinley. It is probable that too many of the delegates remembered some of Reed's barbed comments at their expense. He retired from the House in 1899 and died at Portland in 1902.

*Daniel Webster by
James Henry
Wright.*

Another nationally prominent figure began his professional career in Maine. Daniel Webster became preceptor of Fryeburg Academy in 1802. He wrote: "Nothing here is unpleasant. There is a pretty little society; people treat me with kindness and I have the fortune to find myself in a very good family...." After he left the academy and again took up law studies, Webster defended a case in court at Fryeburg. The Widow Amhead had been sued by John Moss for $15. He claimed the widow owed him this for a heifer.

Unfortunately for Webster, the judge was his own father, Judge Ebenezer Webster, and the young Webster became completely confused. To close the defense, he turned to the court and said, "Your Honor, I never should have taken this case. Only a good lawyer could have won it. My client owes the $15, but I shall pay the $15 myself because I've failed the poor woman. The poor woman has toiled as no man in our hard working community has toiled. I'll pay it because it is unendurable that any woman should struggle as Mrs. Amhead has struggled and go down defeated by a mean man's cupidity."

This brought Moss to his feet, shouting, "Dang it! I don't want the money. All I want is an admission it was owed me. I'm satisfied, but you're the worst lawyer I ever heard, Dan Webster. All you have is a voice." In later years rapt attention was to be paid to that great voice throughout the land.

An early figure of great glamor played a part in Maine's history. This was Antoine de la Mothe Cadillac. Many know him as the founder of Detroit, while others are familiar with his work in helping to build the state of Missouri. Not many know, however, that the French nobleman once owned Mount Desert Island and lived on it at one time. Cadillac Mountain takes its name from him.

Another early New England leader, William Phips, was born in Maine in 1651. As a boy he was a ship's carpenter, and later went to sea to begin amassing his fortune by treasure hunting. He was knighted by Britain and became the first royal governor of Massachusetts. He has been called "America's first self-made man."

A later governor was Percival P. Baxter. As a young man he was greatly impressed with the wonder and value of the wilderness region surrounding Mount Katahdin. Through five legislative sessions and two terms as governor, he worked unsuccessfully to have the region put aside as a state park.

Returning to private life after his career in government service, Baxter bought a 6,690-acre (2,707-hectare) tract, including most of the mountain, and deeded it to the state with the understanding that "it be held by the State as Trustee, in Trust for the benefit of the People of Maine, forever left in its natural wild state, forever be kept as a sanctuary for wild beasts and birds and forever be used for public forest, public park and public recreational purposes." Since that time, the largest part of the expanded 200,000-acre (80,973-hectare) park has been the portion donated by Baxter.

Prominent Maine military men include Commander Edward Preble, conqueror of the Barbary Pirates; Henry Knox, a hero of Bunker Hill and friend and secretary of war of George Washington; and General Joshua Chamberlain, Congressional Medal of Honor winner, president of Bowdoin College, and governor of Maine.

SUCH INTERESTING PEOPLE

Cyrus H.K. Curtis, founder of the mammoth Curtis Publishing Company, was born in Portland in 1850. He gave to the city the splendid Kotzschmar organ at City Hall, in memory of his music teacher, Herman Kotzschmar. Another noted publisher from Maine was George Palmer Putnam, who founded the book publishing firm of G.P. Putnam's Sons.

Charles Albert Coffin, who established the mammoth General Electric Company, was born in Somerset County in 1844.

The eminent Maxim brothers were born in Maine—Hudson Maxim at Boyd Lake in 1853 and Hiram at Sangerville in 1840. Hiram Maxim was the inventor of the machine gun. Hudson Maxim was recognized for his pioneer work in new explosives.

Another notable Maine family was that of Israel Washburn and his seven sons—Israel, Jr., a governor of Maine; William D., prominent manufacturer and senator from Minnesota; Samuel, Civil War ship captain; Charles, minister to Paraguay from the United States; Cadwallader, manufacturer and banker and Union army general and later governor of Wisconsin; Elihu, Grant's secretary of state and minister to France; and Algernon, banker and merchant.

Among the prominent Maine natives of Indian descent are the Sockalexis brothers. Andrew was a member of the 1912 Olympic team, and his brother Louis played for the Cleveland American League baseball team. In fact, it was because of the colorful Indian player that the Cleveland team came to be known as the Indians.

The Indian leader Joseph Orono is credited with saving Maine for this country by persuading his men to assist the European settlers against the Mohawks. When he died in 1801, he was supposed to be 113 years old. The town of Orono is named in his memory. One of the most respected American Indians was Aspinquid, a convert of John Eliot. Aspinquid worked almost without rest to spread Christianity and preach to the tribes throughout New England. He is sometimes known as Saint Aspinquid.

Nescambiou, of Pequowket (Fryeburg), was the only Indian ever to be knighted by the French. For his bravery in the French and Indian wars, he was invited to France to receive the honor.

Another who labored for Christianity was Parson Smith, who served as a minister at Portland for seventy years.

One of the most famous residents of the Portland area was Arctic explorer and discoverer of the South Pole Admiral Robert E. Peary. His home was located on picturesque Eagle Island.

Charles Gulick was a pioneer in physical education. He founded what is said to be the first girls' camp of its kind in the United States. He later helped to create the game of basketball. Gulick and his wife also established the Campfire Girls, a national organization.

One of the unusual incidents of Maine history involved merchant captain Samuel Clough. No one is quite sure of the details, but Captain Clough took part in a plan to rescue Queen Marie Antoinette of France from prison. Some of her belongings were smuggled on board a ship, to be used by the queen on her way to America, but of course she was executed before the plan could be carried out.

The queen's possessions were held by the Cloughs for years, and many romantic tales have been told about them. It was said that a brilliant robe of the king of France was made into a handsome dress by Mrs. Clough. Captain Clough had another rather eccentric distinction: he allegedly introduced the unusual coon cat into Maine.

Tales of the great strength of Barney Beal are still told on the island that bears his name—Beals Island. He was six feet, seven inches (200 centimeters) tall. In one feat of strength he knocked over a horse when the animal's driver guided him too close. At another time, while fishing in his boat, Barney was attacked by British sailors. He took away their guns, broke them over his knee, and threw them back into their boat; when they kept up with the attack, he grabbed one by the arm, snapping the bone like a wishbone. At another time Beal won a fight with fifteen men in a tavern.

Teaching and Learning

One of the nation's outstanding institutions of higher education is Bowdoin College at Brunswick, founded in 1794. In proportion to its size (about 1,400 students) it has had a large number of distinguished graduates. In addition to Henry Wadsworth Longfellow and Hawthorne, already mentioned in connection with the college, the list includes Admiral Robert E. Peary, Arctic explorer Donald B. MacMillan, Thomas B. Reed, William P. Frye, Hannibal Hamlin, and President Franklin Pierce—among many others.

An interesting Bowdoin College tradition concerns Henry Wadsworth Longfellow and Franklin Pierce, who attended Bowdoin at the same time and were personal friends. Pierce drank rather heavily, and on one occasion after Longfellow had put Pierce to bed after a drinking bout, Longfellow said, "Frank, if you are ever going to be president of the United States you will have to stop drinking." Pierce is reported to have stopped drinking and, of course, he did become president of the United States.

One of the interesting events in the college's history occurred during its fiftieth anniversary celebration when alumnus and former professor Longfellow returned to read his *Morituri, Te Salutamus.*

Dominating the small town of Orono is the University of Maine, with more than twice as many students as the population of the town. When the university opened in 1868, it was one of the original land grant colleges, specializing in agriculture. When students did not have money to pay their tuition, they were sometimes permitted to use commodities, such as cords of wood. In 1897 its courses were broadened, and it became the University of Maine.

At Orono, the university occupies a 500-acre (202-hectare) campus, modern in every way. As might be expected, its school of forestry is particularly noteworthy. Work in agricultural fields still is an important part of the curriculum. Highmore Farm is an outstanding 300-acre (121-hectare) experimental farm run by the university.

The University of Maine also has campuses at Farmington, Fort Kent, Machias, Portland-Gorham, and Presque Isle. It also maintains branches at Augusta and Bangor.

Colby College, Waterville

Although the school was founded in 1813, the Georgian style buildings on the 850-acre (344-hectare) campus of highly selective Colby College at Waterville all are quite new and up-to-date. Graduates of the college have gained particular distinction in education. When a survey was taken many years ago, even at that time the alumni included thirty-nine college presidents, six of whom were founders of colleges.

A part of the history of Colby College is the strange travels of the college bell. The bell was cast in the Paul Revere foundry in 1824. As a prank some students took it from its belfry in South College building and shipped it to Harvard University—collect. To carry on the prank, the Harvard students shipped it collect to the University of Virginia. The students there thought it would be a good trick to send it collect to Queen Victoria of England. Colby College authorities caught up with their prize bell just as it was resting on the pier awaiting shipment across the ocean.

Bates College at Lewiston pioneered in college training for women on the same basis as for men. It grew out of the Maine State Seminary, which had been founded by Free Baptists in 1855. When the school became Bates College in 1864, it also became coeducational. Large numbers of its graduates have gone into educational work.

One of Maine's pioneering efforts in education is of particular interest. In 1823 Robert H. Gardiner established a technical school at Gardiner. This is said to be the first school of science and engineering ever established in an English-speaking country. Benjamin Hale, head of the school, said of the students, "They must be made acquainted with machines." Unfortunately, the school lost its state aid and was forced to close. Although Rensselaer Polytechnic Institute of Troy, New York, was founded a year after the Gardiner Lyceum, the New York institution is usually considered the first technical school.

Among four-year Maine colleges are Westbrook College, Portland; Ricker College, Houlton; Thomas College, Waterville; St. Joseph's College, North Windham; Nasson College, Springvale; Bangor Theological Seminary; Maine Maritime Academy, Castine; St. Francis College, Biddeford; and Husson College, Bangor.

The first educational efforts in Maine to merit the name "school" were carried on by Father Sebastian Rasle. He set up his mission school at Kennebec in 1696. Today a state board of education of ten members administers the state laws relating to education. Under the School Administrative District Law, smaller towns with separate school districts are encouraged to merge into larger districts to provide better education and more economical operation.

Enchantment of Maine

"Maine today is as fabulously exciting and unique as ever it was in its legendary past," is the extravagant claim of the Maine State Development Office. The speaker points to the great contrasts. Those who prefer a canoe trip in a wilderness setting and those who want clambakes over a driftwood fire can both be satisfied; in fact, they can even enjoy both recreations on the same day. Fine mountain climbing and calm rides on a ferry or passenger boat among idyllic islands are both available.

For scenery lovers, picturesque white New England churches dot the countryside. One of the ten covered bridges remaining in Maine

Congregational Church, York.

might appear around the corner. Autumn colors are so brilliant that those who see color pictures of the Maine foliage are sure the colors must be exaggerated. The flame of maple, the gold of the birch glittering through the snow white bark, and the deep emerald of the evergreens all combine to make an autumn wonderland. Maine's snows are among the world's most perfect for skiing. Ice skating, ice fishing, and tobaganning are popular winter sports.

In spring, fields of wildflowers herald a coming summer season in which woodland theaters and music camps offer additional Maine attractions. Maine was the leader in summer camps for children, and sporting camps offer adults unique wilderness opportunities.

All of these activities have been carefully and professionally arranged. Detailed instructions for following dozens of canoe trips—from rugged to easy—are available. The same is true of many mountain-climbing expeditions. Each mountain has been graded according to its interest and the difficulty of reaching the top. The best areas for fishing, hunting, and other activities are well documented.

Maine guides are among the most famous in the world. There is even a Maine Junior Guides program for young people. After long and careful study of the wilderness, would-be junior guides are put through a three-day testing program. Those who pass are awarded their certificates by the governor.

Although Maine prides itself on having one of the last true wilderness areas remaining in the eastern United States, it has all of the history of the other New England states. Old homes, antique treasures, and forts are remnants of past struggles, reminders of the famous and not so famous who devoted their lives to the state.

MACHIGONNE—CASCO—FALMOUTH—PORTLAND

In 1882 the citizens of Portland gathered to dedicate the city's first civic monument and to recall the city's historic past which the monument on the promenade commemorates. This was erected in memory of the two founders of the city, Richard Tucker and George Cleve. On the base are the four names by which the city has been known—Machigonne, Casco, Falmouth, and finally Portland, last name becoming official on July 4, 1786.

The four names recall the history of the community that was destroyed three times and rebuilt after Indian attack, war, and a terrible fire. Many reminders of that history may still be seen. Among these is the old observatory which served for 116 years as a watchtower for incoming ships and for spotting distress at sea.

Portland Head Lighthouse, finished in 1790, was the first lighthouse to be authorized by the federal government. The poet Longfellow spent many hours at the base of Portland Head Light.

The poet recalled another historic Portland landmark in "My Lost Youth":

> I remember the bulwarks by the shore,
> And the fort upon the hill;
> The sunrise gun, with its hollow roar,
> The drum-beat repeated o'er and o'er,
> And the bugle wild and shrill.

This referred to old Fort Allen, hastily built in 1814 for protection in the War of 1812.

Beautiful island-dotted Casco Bay provides the setting for modern Portland. Almost every island in the bay has its own tales of history and romance. Boat trips are available for visitors who want to explore the islands. Some of the islands, such as Long Island, have excellent roads. Because of the many pirates who operated in the region, there are innumerable stories of buried treasure, and treasure hunters never seem to tire of searching for lost riches.

One of the most persistent stories involves the legendary wealth of Captain Kidd on Jewell Island. The fact that Kidd probably never visited the region hardly seems to bother the eager searchers. One story states that a stranger once appeared asking for the help of a captain. It was said that the stranger later disappeared mysteriously, and the captain soon flashed sudden wealth.

Littlejohn Island was an Indian camping ground, and some particularly fine Indian relics are found there, along with great heaps of shells discarded by Indian feasters.

Portland is fortunate to have another attractive region just to the northwest. Few communities of its size are so close to all the charms of the great outdoors. Sebago Lake is one of the country's great resort areas—a vast playground of the East. This must have been true in prehistoric times as well; the Indian burial ground on the shores of Sebago Lake is one of the largest in the country.

Nathaniel Hawthorne lived at Raymond and spent much time in the Sebago region. He wrote: "I have visited many places called beautiful in Europe and the United States but have never seen the place that enchanted me like the flat rock from which I used to fish."

Pulpit Rock on the shore of the lake was often used by Indian chiefs to address their people. A Captain Frye had been pursued by Indians for several miles. He leaped from the rock into the lake and found an underwater cave in which to hide. At night he swam over to the large island that bears his name. Hawthorne is said to have written the beginning pages of his *The Scarlet Letter* in the cave where Frye hid.

Another cave near the lake is supposedly the place where Indian captors hid a 14-year-old girl for three years. At last, her family discovered the hiding place and rescued her.

There are many tourist attractions within Portland. As early as 1836, it was suggested that scenic drives could be built to follow the heights on both sides of the city. Two spectacular promenades resulted—eastern and western—providing panoramic views of the bay and harbor.

The present City Hall is the third to be built in Portland. Constructed of Maine granite, it is the home of the famous Kotzschmar Memorial Organ, said to be one of the largest and finest anywhere. Frequent recitals are presented to the public.

The city's museums include the Portland Museum of Art, housed in Lorenzo de Medici Sweat Mansion. It features work of Maine artists. There is the interesting Museum of Natural History, and the Maine Historical Society has a museum exhibiting objects from the precolonial period.

Among the interesting old houses open to visitors are the Victoria Mansion, filled with relics of its period, and the Wadsworth-

Portland's City Hall is constructed of Maine granite.

Longfellow House, housing mementos of the poet. The Wadsworth-Longfellow House is maintained by the Maine Historical Society. The large bronze statue of Longfellow by Franklin Simmons stands in Longfellow Square. Names of schoolchildren who contributed money to finance the statue are housed in the pedestal of the monument. Other Portland monuments include the Reed monument, a tribute to Thomas B. Reed, and the U.S.S. *Portland* monument, the main mast and bridge of the historic World War II ship. An even more historic ship is represented by one of its guns mounted in Fort Allen Park. The people of the state, and of the country, remember the battleship *Maine* which was blown up in Havanna harbor in 1898, signalling the start of the Spanish-American War.

Monument Square in downtown Portland commemorates the more than five thousand Portland soldiers and sailors who served in the Civil War. It was dedicated in 1891. The bronze statues were done by the sculptor Simmons, a native of the state.

First Parish Church is considered the oldest public building of stone in Maine. Another notable church building is the Cathedral of the Immaculate Conception. The wood carving in St. Luke's Cathedral was executed by the German carver Kirschmeyer, one of the finest such craftsmen.

SEAT OF GOVERNMENT

Maine's imposing statehouse in Augusta rises with majesty to the full height of its 185-foot (56-meter) dome, made of copper, topped with the gold leaf-covered statue of Wisdom. One of America's most distinguished architects, Charles Bulfinch, designed the building, completed in 1832. The builders used the fine granite of nearby Hallowell quarry. White Maine marble was also employed.

The original building has been enlarged and expanded several times, but the noble Bulfinch front was preserved. The rotunda is a room of great dignity, featuring eight Doric columns. Plate glass cases display Maine's honored battle flags. The State Museum even encloses a real stream and a twenty-four foot (seven-meter) pool containing some of Maine's finest salmon and trout. A replica of one of the state's historic covered bridge, spans the stream.

The capitol is in spacious State Park, part of the original thirty-four acres (fourteen hectares) of ground conveyed to the state for state buildings. Here also is the fine State House Office Building, built in 1954. The park has been called "one of the most attractive parts of Augusta." The park has an arboretum with a fine collection of trees and plants for study and enjoyment.

In 1919 the daughter of James G. Blaine presented her father's mansion to the state as a memorial to her son, who lost his life in World War I. The house, with its impressive landscaped grounds, is now the governor's mansion. It was here that Blaine, the "Plumed Knight of Politics," learned of his nomination for the presidency and also of his defeat. The house's study has been restored just as it was when James G. Blaine lived there. One of the most prized mementos is the original silver service of the battleship *Maine*. This was recovered from Havana harbor ten years after the *Maine* was sunk there.

The Indians considered the site of Augusta hallowed ground. European settlement began there when the Plymouth colony established a trading outpost in 1628 at the head of navigation of the Kennebec River, forty-eight miles (seventy-seven kilometers) from

State House, Augusta.

open sea; tides of up to four feet (1.2 meters) ebb and flow there. The earliest post there was known as Cushnoc.

The "lustie yonge man" John Howland, who almost lost his life when he was washed overboard from the *Mayflower,* was the leader of the Cushnoc post. John Alden, made famous in Longfellow's *Courtship of Miles Standish,* shared the command.

Fort Western was built on the eastern bank of the river as protection against the Indians. Captain James Howard, the first commander of the fort, is considered to be Augusta's first permanent settler. The historic old fort has been restored. It shows examples of the area's early life, and there are many interesting exhibits.

The ill-fated Benedict Arnold expedition stopped at the site of Augusta. An interesting incident in the life of another infamous character of American history occurred there. Nineteen-year-old Aaron Burr was a member of the Arnold expedition. At Augusta he fell in love with the Indian Princess Jacataqua and made love to her under the Jacataqua Oak. The Princess was being held at Fort Western. Before the Arnold expedition moved on, a great feast was held at the fort; the bear providing meat for the main course had been killed by Burr and the princess.

One of the strange events in Augusta history was the "Malta War." Many squatters had settled in nearby Malta on lands legally claimed by absentee property owners. A surveyor hired by the owners was killed by squatters disguised as Indians. When the killers were jailed, a mob of squatters arrived to free them. Several companies of militia had to be called out, and it was some time before order returned after the prisoners were found not guilty.

The United States Veterans Administration facility near Augusta was the first institution in the country to be established for disabled veterans. It was opened in 1866.

THE REST OF THE SOUTHWEST

Southwestern Maine, near the New Hampshire border, has many interesting areas. The site of old Fort McClary is now a state park.

This fort was built by Massachusetts to protect its rights from encroachment by New Hampshire. In addition to the navy shipyards, the John Paul Jones Memorial and the Lady Pepperell House are points of interest of the Kittery region.

The Gaol (jail) of York is said to be the oldest remaining public building in the East. The Sarah Orne Jewett house, the birthplace of the writer, at South Berwick has a reputation as "one of the finest in New England."

One of the favorite folktales of the South Berwick area concerns the little daughter of General Ichabod Goodwin. When the general left the little girl alone with a servant for a short time, he told her to be courteous to any guests who dropped in. A band of robbers invaded the house, but the courteous little girl ordered the servant to bring tea. She was much puzzled when the guests began to put the silverware in a bag and seize other prize items. However, she refused to be inhospitable, and offered her own silver cup in exchange for the other items. The leader of the robbers ordered his men to put everything back, and they left.

The story continues that later, when the thieves were caught, the general asked the leader why they took nothing at his house. He said that he was touched when he had been treated "for the first time in my life like a gentleman."

Ogunquit is the home of a popular artists' colony. Artists from all over the country exhibit there, and the town has several art museums, as well as a summer playhouse offering "name" actors. North of Ogunquit the rock-bound coast spreads out into a fine long beach. Still farther north, Old Orchard Beach has been a popular resort for more than a century.

The records of the Alfred County Courthouse are a treasure of historic interest extending back as far as 1636.

The Chase House at East Limington was built from plans by Mrs. Chase, who happened to draw them on an eight-sided hat box. The house, of course, is octagon shaped. After construction of the house had started, it was found that Mrs. Chase had neglected to include a stairway, and the plans were altered slightly for this vital addition.

Porter is still the center of worship of the Bullockites, a group of

Screw Auger Falls.

"primitive" Baptists. The few remaining members still worship in their meeting house, which is more than a century old.

In Naples the people once took their politics so seriously that the Republicans and Democrats used separate entrances to public buildings, and in meetings they sat on separate sides. Naples children even sat on separate Republican and Democrat sides of the classroom.

A natural attraction of western Maine is Screw Augur Falls, where swirling waters have worn curious well-like holes in the river ledges. Some of these are as much as 25 feet (7.6 meters) deep. The old

Oxford County Jail at Paris Hill is one of the few examples of Maine's very old stone buildings.

The twin cities of Lewiston and Auburn form the second largest metropolitan concentration in Maine, located thirty miles (forty-eight kilometers) up the Androscoggin River from the sea. Lewiston Falls and dam are especially spectacular when spring rains swell the volume of the river.

An unusual feature of the Bates College campus at Lewiston is Mount David, a rocky knoll offering a spectacular view of the surroundings as far as the Presidential Range of the White Mountains. Stanton Museum of Bates College has one of the finest ornithological collections in the United States, showing several specimens of rare, extinct birds. Lewiston's Stanton Bird Club Sanctuary is a 226-acre (91-hectare) home of interesting feathered creatures.

Poland Spring House, at Poland Spring, was once the largest private resort in New England. The huge hotel is built around the original Mansion House, constructed in 1794. Spring water from the region is bottled and shipped around the world. The Maine State Building, once the Maine building at the Chicago World's Columbian Exposition in 1893, is located at the resort's grounds.

Durham was noted as the center of the religious sect founded by the Reverend Frank W. Sandford. He called his group the Church of the Holy Ghost and Us; it attracted large numbers of followers and became national and international in scope. Followers came from all over the world and contributed their money to a common treasury. Sandford ordered a perpetual vigil in a high tower to prepare for the end of the world. When this failed to come about as predicted, he and many of his followers set out in three white ships for Jerusalem to visit the Holy Land. However, the journey was unsuccessful, and they returned in great want after suffering many hardships.

With flowing beard, purple robe, and sailor hat, Sandford made a spectacular figure on board his sailing vessel, the *Coronet*, carrying out his "commission to convert the heathen." The sect built the unusual and imposing Temple Shiloh and other headquarter buildings between Durham and Freeport.

Brunswick is most noted as the home of Bowdoin College. The

college's Walker Art Gallery is one of the finest small art museums in the country and has served as a model for many others. It houses the art treasures donated to the college by James Bowdoin, son of Massachusetts Governor James Bowdoin, one of the benefactors of the college. The son gathered the first private collection of European art ever made by an American and donated it to Bowdoin College.

The Longfellow Room in the Bowdoin College Library contains one of the most valuable collections concerning the Maine poet, including books and manuscripts. Brunswick Playhouse is a well-known summer theater held in the Packard Theater on the campus.

The Fort Baldwin Memorial and Fort Popham Memorial are both at Popham Beach. Reid State Park is a popular coast playground.

The Indians took twenty beaver skins in payment for the Boothbay Harbor region. Many excursions to the nearby islands are popular. Guides enjoy telling the tale of Squire Greenleaf, who owned and loved Squirrel Island. He had always expressed a desire to be buried in the sand of Davenport Cove on the island. When he died, diggers were sent with a scow to get sand from the cove. Instead of going to the cove, they decided that the first convenient sand would do. On the way back, a storm came up, and several of the crew said the ghost of the squire appeared before them, making angry gestures. When they hurried back and gathered the proper sand, the storm let up, or so the story goes.

Squirrel Island has been the location of a self-governing colony of educators, writers, and other professional persons. Another retreat of artists and writers is isolated Monhegan Island, noted for its fabulous lobster fishing. It was on this island that John Smith first used the term "New England," which eventually was applied to the entire region of the northeast coast.

Five different forts were built at Pemaquid for various purposes. The first was for defense against the pirate Dixie Bull. Bull had been a trader. When his goods were seized by the French at Castine, he became a pirate for revenge. He was among the best known of the buccaneers. His infamous deeds included the sacking of Pemaquid. The last of the four forts, Fort William Henry, has been reconstructed for visitors.

Tenant's Harbor is known for its spouting horn, a trough of stone through which waves sometimes shoot upward as high as forty feet (twelve meters). When the early travel writer Roiser in 1605 saw the region of St. George, he wrote in his *True Relation* that it was the "most beautiful large and secure harboring river that the world affordeth."

Near Warren is the Knox State Arboretum and Academy of Arts and Sciences. The museum has a fine collection of Maine minerals and prehistoric relics. Some authorities believe that Mary Baker Eddy, founder of Christian Science, the Church of Christ, Scientist, and the *Christian Science Monitor,* began her work on *Science and Health with Key to the Scriptures* at Warren.

Clams are still popular at Damariscotta, but probably no more so than they were in ancient days. During that time, an unknown people enjoyed oyster feasts and threw their shells away on a mound which over endless years soon grew to the size of a large hill—a monument to an appetite for shellfish.

Other relics of pre-European times are found in the Waterville region. A large Indian village once stood on the west Kennebec bank where many industries now rise. A very old Indian burial ground was found in the region. The Colby College Library at Waterville houses a fine collection of manuscripts of most of Maine's prominent authors. The original autographed manuscript of Smith's anthem "America" is one of its treasures. Original works by almost all the authors mentioned previously may be found there. The Bixler Art Building contains Paul Aker's bust of Milton, known to readers of Hawthorne's Marble Faun, and a well-known Gilbert Stuart portrait of Washington.

Maine's "state theater" is Lakewood, at Skowhegan, the oldest summer theater in the United States.

When Captain John Smith saw the region where Camden now stands, he described it picturesquely as "under the high mountains of the Penobscot, against whose feet the sea doth beat." Today's visitors are still likely to call it one of the loveliest of resort towns. Camden Hills State Park centers on 1,380-foot (421-meter) Mount Megunticook, from which there is a magnificent view. Camden was one of the first communities to support the Revolution, and it takes its name from Lord Camden, a defender of the colonies in the British Parliament.

Belmont was first settled by squatters. Whenever they heard that lawmen or strangers were coming, they put on Indian costumes, and the town seemed to be entirely inhabited by lounging Indians.

Searsport is known as the home of many naval men. The Penobscot Marine Museum displays a fine collection of early marine exhibits.

At Carmel the Reverend George Higgins founded the Higginsite sect. One of his activities was driving out the devil from children by whipping them. People of the neighborhood grew so incensed at this that they tarred and feathered the whipping pastor and drove him from the town.

Another sect was founded in the nearby town of Hermon. The Millerites were disciples of William Miller. He also won many followers by preaching that the end of the world would soon come. His people gave away all their property and on a day in 1843 they anointed themselves and waited all day looking at the sky. Although, of course, nothing happened, many groups remained loyal to Miller until his death.

EASTERN MAINE

Bangor, the metropolis of eastern Maine, is nicknamed The Queen City. Its distinctive name came to it through an odd mistake. The Reverend Seth Noble, an early pastor, went to Boston to apply for incorporation for the town. While he was waiting, he hummed the old hymn tune "Bangor." The clerk, filling out the incorporation papers, asked him the name of the town; the pastor thought he had asked him the name of the tune, and replied, "Bangor." And so the name Bangor was written into the incorporation papers, and the city has been Bangor ever since. One of the points of interest is the giant 31-foot (9.4-meter) tall statue of Paul Bunyan.

Bucksport was settled in 1764; however, it was so severely

Paul Bunyan statue in Bangor.

destroyed by the British in 1779 that the town was not resettled until 1812. Its leading industry is newsprint. The register of the Jed Prouty Tavern showed the bold signatures of such famous persons as Andrew Jackson, William Harrison, and John Tyler.

Historic Castine was the center for almost two hundred years of struggle for the ownership of the region. The British held it during the Revolution and Paul Revere's military career ended there when he failed in an attempt to recapture it. Fort George has been under the flags of four nations—France, England, The Netherlands, and the United States. There are many historic houses and a museum at Castine, and the Maine Maritime Academy is located there. It operates the S.S. *State of Maine* for training maritime personnel.

Most of Acadia National Park is on beautiful Mount Desert Island; the remainder is partly on the mainland and partly on Isle au Haut. Bar Harbor, long the summer home of the wealthy and socially

Winter in Acadia National Park.

elite, is the largest town on the island, which is now reached by bridge from the mainland. Adding to the island's beauty and interest is the fact that the northern and temperate floral zones meet in Acadia National Park, and an almost bewildering variety of blooms and plants are protected there.

For years the ferry *Bluenose* carried 600 passengers and 150 cars on a seven-hour trip between Bar Harbor and Yarmouth, Nova Scotia.

At Jonesport, G.J. Adams organized the Palestine Emigration Association. His followers sold their possessions and made arrangements to sail to Palestine, where 175 of them founded a community. Disagreements and difficulties finally caused the colony to break up and those who were left returned to the United States.

For almost one hundred years, until 1750, the site of Machias was called a "pirates' nest" because of the number of pirates operating in the region. Pirate Samuel Bellamy made his headquarters there and even built a crude fort. He was called the Robin Hood of Atlantic Pirates.

West Lubec and Pembroke are both known for their rather unusual natural attractions; each has "reversing" falls. The waters tumble one way when the tide is going out and cascade in the other direction when the tide reverses. Campobello Island, summer home of President Franklin D. Roosevelt, is reached from Lubec, although it is part of Canada rather than Maine.

The Roosevelt Campobello International Park is unique in its administration. In accordance with the intergovernmental agreement and legislative action of both countries, the park is administered by a joint United States-Canadian Roosevelt Campobello International Park Commission, consisting of three Canadian and three United States members.

International cooperation is heartily practiced by the Maine town of Calais and its neighbor, St. Stephen, New Brunswick, just across the St. Croix River. Calais operates the library and in turn gets its water supply from Canada. It may be the only city in the world to "import" its entire water supply. Calais was named for the city in France, in honor of the French assistance given the country during the Revolution. The people of the two cities still exchange gifts on occasion.

THE VAST AND STIMULATING NORTH

One of the few remaining areas of almost unspoiled wilderness in the United States is found in northwestern Maine. There is not a single town on the Maine side of the northwest border with Canada. Part of State Route 27 is known as the Arnold Trail, because it follows closely the route taken by Arnold's Revolutionary army. Much of the region is completely without roads, and the innumerable streams and lakes provide the "highways."

Mount Katahdin and Moosehead Lake are the area's top attractions. The town of Greenville is the gateway to enormous Moosehead area and the sprawling wilderness surrounding it. Eleven miles (eighteen kilometers) north of Greenville is Lily Bay State Park, on the shores of the lake. Here is some of the best fishing in the state. The poet John Greenleaf Whittier wrote his poem "To a Pine Tree" after a visit to Moosehead Lake.

Mount Katahdin stands in scenic domination of a vast area of smaller peaks, lakes, streams, and endless forests, forever preserved for the people through the generosity of Percival P. Baxter. Mount Katahdin holds a number of unusual records. From its highest point, more land and water can be seen than from any other point in the United States. It is also claimed that more literature has been written about Mount Katahdin than about any other United States peak.

When Henry David Thoreau, the famed naturalist, climbed the mountain in 1846 he wrote: "The surrounding world looked as if a huge mirror had been shattered, and glittering bits thrown on the grass," referring to the multitude of lakes and ponds shining in the sun in every direction.

Meadows of Alpine flowers, Arctic plants which have survived there since the Ice Ages, carpet the slopes of Mount Katahdin—Alpine holy-grass, narrow-leaved Labrador tea, fir clubmoss, Lapland rosebay, Greenland starwort, Lapland diapensia, trailing azalea, and others.

Mount Katahdin is the northern terminal of the long Appalachian Trail, which winds across the crest of the eastern mountains from south to north.

Such challenges as this rugged trail are especially appropriate in a state where the sturdy people have always been alert to every challenge to the individual dignity and freedom which they cherish so greatly.

Opposite: Mount Katahdin.

Handy Reference Section

Instant Facts

Became the 23rd state March 15, 1820
Capital—Augusta, settled 1628
Nickname—Pine Tree State
Motto—*Dirigo* ("I Direct")
State bird—Chickadee *(Parus atricapillus)*
State fish—Landlocked salmon
State tree—Eastern white pine *(Pinus strobus linnaeus)*
State flower—Cone and tassel of white pine
State mineral—Tourmaline
State song—"State of Maine Song," by Roger Vinton Snow
Area—33,215 square miles (86,026 square kilometers)
Rank in area—39th
Greatest length (north to south)—320 miles (515 kilometers)
Greatest width (east to west)—210 miles (338 kilometers)
Highest point—5,267 feet (1,605 meters), Mount Katahdin
Lowest point—Sea level
Geographic center—Piscataquis (18 miles [29 kilometers] north of Dover)
Population—1,099,000 (1980 projection)
Population rank in nation—38th
Population density—33 per square mile (12.7 per square kilometers)
Physicians per 100,000—121

Principal cities—		
Portland	65,116	(1970 census)
Lewiston	41,779	
Bangor	33,168	
Auburn	24,151	
South Portland	23,267	
Augusta	21,945	

You Have a Date with History

1497—The Cabots sail along coast
1524—Verrazano explores
1525—Gomes visits Penobscot region
1569—English sailors traverse Maine
1580—John Walker leads expedition to Penobscot region
1602—Gosnold takes furs, cedar, and sassafras back to England
1604—First European settlement (St. Croix)
1605—Waymouth kidnaps five Indians
1607—Popham settlement (St. George); first ship constructed by English in New World

90

1622—First permanent settlement (Monhegan)
1652—Maine comes under Massachusetts jurisdiction
1675—King Philip's War begins in Maine
1688—King William's War
1690—Only four settlements in Maine remain inhabited
1691—Sir William Phips appointed royal governor of Massachusetts
1703—Queen Anne's War begins
1722—Lovewell's War (fourth Indian war)
1744—King George's War begins (fifth Indian war)
1754—Sixth Indian war begins
1760—Peace reigns after the Indian wars
1775—Revolutionary War comes to Maine
1791—Portland Head Lighthouse established (oldest on Atlantic coast)
1794—Bowdoin College chartered
1812—Maine suffers another war
1820—Statehood
1832—Augusta becomes capital
1842—Boundary dispute finally settled
1865—Maine had contributed 72,942 men to Civil War
1898—Battleship *Maine* blown up at Havana; war begins
1918—Maine had contributed more than 35,000 men in World War I
1935—Passamaquoddy Tidal Power Project begins
1945—More than 95,000 men and women of Maine served in World War II
1964—Maine votes for Lyndon B. Johnson for president
1969—Personal and corporate income taxes are adopted
1974—Voters elect first Independent governor in modern times
1977—Justice department supports Indian land claims.

Thinkers, Doers, Fighters

People of renown who have been associated with Maine

Abbott, Jacob
Blaine, James G.
Browne, Charles Farrar
  (Artemus Ward)
Carroll, Gladys Hasty
Cary, Annie Louise
Coffin, Charles Albert
Coffin, Robert P. Tristram
Curtis, Cyrus H.K.
Fuller, Melville W.
Furlong, Atherton
Hamlin, Hannibal
Hawthorne, Nathaniel
Homer, Winslow

Kellogg, Elijah
Kent, Rockwell
Knox, Henry
Longfellow, Henry Wadsworth
Lovejoy, Elijah
Macmillan, Donald
Millay, Edna St. Vincent
Maxim, Hiram
Maxim, Hudson
Nordica, Lillian
Nye, Edgar Wilson (Bill)
Paine, John Knowles
Patten, Gilbert
Peary, Robert E.

Pierce, Franklin
Preble, Edward
Putnam, George Palmer
Reed, Thomas Brackett
Roberts, Kenneth
Robinson, Edwin Arlington
Smith, Margaret Chase
Smith, Samuel Francis

Stanley Brothers
Standish, Bert L.
Stowe, Harriet Beecher
Vallee, Rudy
Webster, Daniel
Whittier, John Greenleaf
Wiggins, Kate Douglas
Willis, Nathaniel Parker

Governors of the State

William King 1820-1821
William D. Williamson 1821
Benjamin Ames 1821-1822
Albion K. Parris 1822-1827
Enoch Lincoln 1827-1829
Nathan Cutler 1829
Joshua Hall 1830
Jonathan G. Hunton 1830-1831
Samuel E. Smith 1831-1834
Robert P. Dunlap 1834-1838
Edward Kent 1838-1839
John Fairfield 1839-1841
Edward Kent 1841-1842
John Fairfield 1842-1843
Edw. Kavanaugh 1843-1844
Hugh J. Anderson 1844-1847
John W. Dana 1847-1850
John Hubbard 1850-1853
William G. Crosby 1853-1855
Anson P. Morrill 1855-1856
Samuel Wells 1856-1857
Hannibal Hamlin 1857
Jos. H. Williams 1857-1858
Lot M. Morrill 1858-1861
Israel Washburn, Jr. 1861-1863
Abner Coburn 1863-1864
Samuel Cony 1864-1867
Joshua L. Chamberlain 1867-1871
Sidney Perham 1871-1874
Nelson Dingley, Jr. 1874-1876
Seldon Connor 1876-1879
Alonzo Garcelon 1879-1880

Daniel F. Davis 1880-1881
Harris M. Plaisted 1881-1883
Frederick Robie 1883-1887
Joseph R. Bodwell 1887
S.S. Marble 1887-1889
Edwin C. Burleigh 1889-1893
Henry B. Cleaves 1893-1897
Llewellyn Powers 1897-1901
John Fremont Hill 1901-1905
William T. Cobb 1905-1909
Bert M. Fernald 1909-1911
Frederick W. Plaisted 1911-1913
William T. Haines 1913-1915
Oakley C. Curtis 1915-1917
Carl E. Milliken 1917-1921
Frederic H. Parkhurst 1921
Percival P. Baxter 1921-1925
Ralph O. Brewster 1925-1929
William Tudor Gardiner 1929-1933
Louis J. Brann 1933-1937
Lewis O. Barrows 1937-1941
Sumner Sewall 1941-1945
Horace Hildreth 1945-1949
Frederick G. Payne 1949-1953
Burton M. Cross 1953-1955
Edmund S. Muskie 1955-1959
Robert N. Haskell 1959
Clinton A. Clauson 1959-1960
John H. Reed 1960-1967
Kenneth Curtis 1967-1975
James B. Longley 1975-1979
Joseph Brennan 1979-

92

Index

95

PICTURE CREDITS

ABOUT THE AUTHOR

With the publication of his first book for school use when he was twenty, **Allan Carpenter** began a career as an author that has spanned more than 135 books. After teaching in the public schools of Des Moines, Mr. Carpenter began his career as an educational publisher at the age of twenty-one when he founded the magazine *Teachers Digest*. In the field of educational periodicals, he was responsible for many innovations. During his many years in publishing, he has perfected a highly organized approach to handling large volumes of factual material: after extensive traveling and having collected all possible materials, he systematically reviews and organizes everything. From his apartment high in Chicago's John Hancock Building, Allan recalls, "My collection and assimilation of materials on the states and countries began before the publication of my first book." Allan is the founder of Carpenter Publishing House and of Infordata International, Inc., publishers of *Issues in Education* and *Index to U. S. Government Periodicals*. When he is not writing or traveling, his principal avocation is music. He has been the principal bassist of many symphonies, and he managed the country's leading non-professional symphony for twenty-five years.